Contents

Grade 7

1. Number Theory .... 2 - 5
2. Algebraic Expressions .... 6 - 9
3. Fractions .... 10 - 13
4. Percent .... 14 - 17
5. Measurement .... 18 - 23
6. Approximation .... 24 - 25
7. Integers .... 26 - 29
8. Fractions, Decimals and Percent .... 30 - 33
   Midway Test .... 34 - 39
9. Coordinates .... 40 - 43
10. More about Algebraic Expressions .... 44 - 49
11. Angles and Lines .... 50 - 53
12. Angles and Shapes .... 54 - 57
13. Statistics .... 58 - 61
14. Transformations .... 62 - 63
15. Probability .... 64 - 65
    Final Test .... 66 - 72

1 Number Theory

WORDS TO LEARN

Power — a product of equal factors
Base (in a power) — the factor repeated in a power
Exponent (in a power) — the number of times the base occurs as a factor

e.g. $2 \times 2 \times 2 \times 2 \times 2 = 2^5 = 32$; 2^5 is called a power. (base = 2, exponent = 5)
In writing, it is two to the fifth power.

Square number — the product of a number multiplied by itself
Square root — one of the two equal factors of a number

Follow Tony's method to write each product as a power and state the base and exponent of each power.

$\underset{1}{4} \times \underset{2}{4} \times \underset{3}{4} \times \underset{4}{4} \times \underset{5}{4} \times \underset{6}{4} = 4^6$
Exponent = 6, Base = 4

Six 4s have been multiplied. 4^6 is the product of six 4s.

① $2 \times 2 \times 2 = \underline{2^3}$ Exponent = __3__   Base = __2__

② $7 \times 7 \times 7 \times 7 \times 7 = \underline{7^5}$ Exponent = __5__   Base = __7__

③ Nine to the sixth power = $\underline{9^6}$ Exponent = __6__   Base = __9__

④ Five to the eighth power = $\underline{5^8}$ Exponent = __8__   Base = __5__

Simplify each power.

⑤ $5^4 = \underline{625}$ ⑥ $3^0 = \underline{1}$ ⑦ $9^1 = \underline{9}$

⑧ $12^2 = \underline{144}$ ⑨ $4^3 = \underline{64}$ ⑩ $8^0 = \underline{1}$

⑪ $13^1 = \underline{13}$ ⑫ $7^0 = \underline{1}$ ⑬ $6^3 = \underline{216}$

A number to the zero power is one.
A number to the first power is itself.
e.g. $2^0 = 1$, $4^1 = 4$

Read what Tony says. Then write each product as a power of 10.

There are about 10^4 people in the parade.

4 tens are multiplied.

$10^4 = 10 \times 10 \times 10 \times 10$
$= 10\,000 \rightarrow$ 1 is followed by 4 zeros.

⑭ $10 \times 10 = \underline{10^2}$ ✓

⑮ $10 \times 10 \times 10 \times 10 \times 10 = \underline{10^5}$ ✓

⑯ $10 \times 10 \times 10 = \underline{10^3}$ ✓

⑰ $10 \times 10 \times 10 \times 10 = \underline{10^4}$ ✓

⑱ one million = $\underline{10^6}$ ✓

⑲ one hundred thousand = $\underline{10^5}$ ✓

⑳ $10 \times 10 \times 10 \times 10 \times 10 \times 10 \times 10 = \underline{10^7}$ ✓

Follow Tony's method to express each number as powers of 10.

$9\,806 = 9000 + 800 + 0 + 6$
$= 9 \times 1000 + 8 \times 100 + 0 \times 10 + 6 \times 1$
$= 9 \times 10^3 + 8 \times 10^2 + 0 \times 10^1 + 6 \times 10^0$

There are 9 806 people in the parade.

㉑ $1\,463 = \underline{1} \times 10^3 + \underline{4} \times 10^2 + \underline{6} \times 10^1 + \underline{3} \times 10^0$ ✓

㉒ $3\,075 = \underline{3 \times 10^3 + 7 \times 10^1 + 5 \times 10^0}$ ✓

㉓ $159 = \underline{1 \times 10^2 + 5 \times 10^1 + 9 \times 10^0}$ ✓

㉔ $42\,062 = \underline{4 \times 10^4 + 2 \times 10^3 + 0 \times 10^2 + 6 \times 10^1 + 2 \times 10^0}$ ✓

Find the value.

㉕ $2 \times 10^4 + 1 \times 10^3 + 4 \times 10^2 + 3 \times 10^1 + 2 \times 10^0 = \underline{21\,432}$ ✓
(20000, 1000, 400, 30, 2)

㉖ $3 \times 10^4 + 5 \times 10^2 + 9 \times 10^0 = \underline{30\,509}$ ✓
(30000, 500, 9)

㉗ $6 \times 10^5 + 3 \times 10^2 + 3 \times 10^1 + 2 \times 10^0 = \underline{60,332}$ (600332)
(600000, 300, 30, 2)

㉘ $4 \times 10^4 + 3 \times 10^2 + 5 \times 10^0 = \underline{40,305}$ ✓
(40,000, 300, 5)

Complete the factor trees and write each number as a product of prime factors.

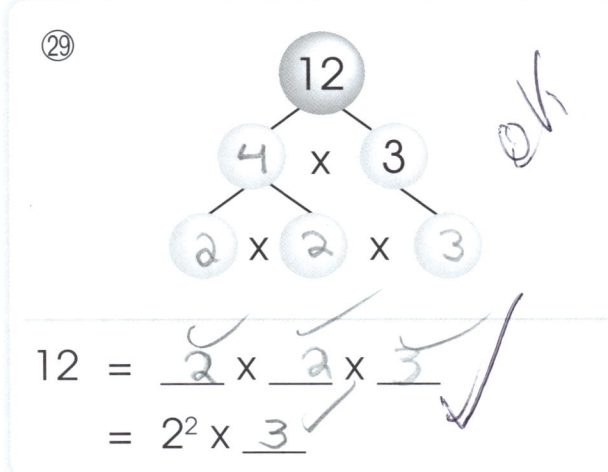

㉙
12 = 2 × 2 × 3
  = 2^2 × 3

㉚
36 = 2 × 2 × 3 × 3
  = 2^2 × 3^2

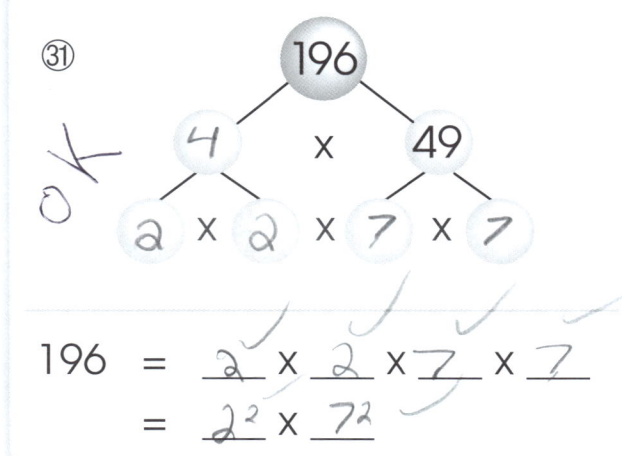

㉛
196 = 2 × 2 × 7 × 7
   = 2^2 × 7^2

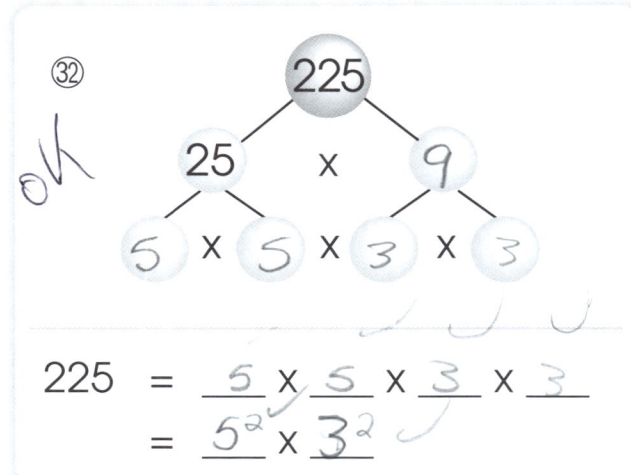

㉜
225 = 5 × 5 × 3 × 3
   = 5^2 × 3^2

Find the prime factors of each number and write as a power.

㉝ 81 = 3^4 ok

㉞ 147 = 3 × 7^2 ok

㉟ 64 = 2^6 ok

㊱ 75 = 3 × 5^2 ok

㊲ 400 = 10^2

㊳ 120 = _____

㊴ 484 = _____

㊵ 72 = _____

㊶ 375 = _____

㊷ 200 = _____

Continue to factorize each composite number until all factors are prime factors.

Follow Tony's method to find the square root of each number.

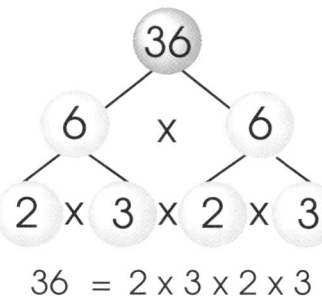

square root of 36:

$\sqrt{36} = \sqrt{2^2 \times 3^2}$
$= \sqrt{(2 \times 3) \times (2 \times 3)}$
$= 2 \times 3$
$= 6$

36 is a square number. 6 is the square root of 36.

㊸ 16 = ___ x ___ x ___ x ___
$\sqrt{16}$ = _____

㊹ 441 = ___ x ___ x ___ x ___
$\sqrt{441}$ = _____

㊺ 100 = ___ x ___ x ___ x ___
$\sqrt{100}$ = _____

㊻ 484 = ___ x ___ x ___ x ___
$\sqrt{484}$ = _____

Use the product of prime factors to find the square root.

㊼ 256 = 2^8
$\sqrt{256}$ = _____

㊽ 900 = $2^2 \times 3^2 \times 5^2$
$\sqrt{900}$ = _____

㊾ 144 = $2^4 \times 3^2$
$\sqrt{144}$ = _____

㊿ 324 = $2^2 \times 3^4$
$\sqrt{324}$ = _____

ACTIVITY

See how Tony arranges his marbles. Then use his clue to predict each sum, without adding.

1 4 9 16

1 1+2+1 1+2+3+2+1 1+2+3+4+3+2+1

1. 1 + 2 + 3 + 4 + 5 + 4 + 3 + 2 + 1 = _____
2. 1 + 2 + 3 + 4 + 5 + 6 + 7 + 6 + 5 + 4 + 3 + 2 + 1 = _____

2 Algebraic Expressions

WORDS TO LEARN

Equation - a mathematical sentence with an equal sign (=)

Follow Tony's method to write the expressions and answer the questions.

> I have 4 in the fridge and y cases of coke in the basement. How many cans of coke do I have if 1 case has 24 cans?
>
> Number of = $24y + 4$
>
> If I have 6 cases, how many cans of coke do I have?
>
> Number of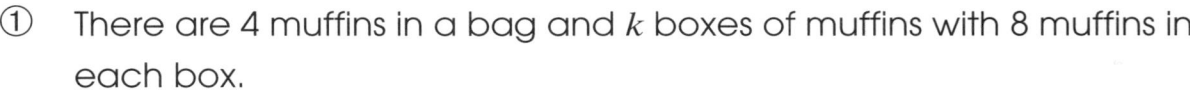

① There are 4 muffins in a bag and k boxes of muffins with 8 muffins in each box.

   a. How many muffins are there?
      Number of muffins = _____

   b. If there are 7 boxes, how many muffins are there?
      Number of muffins = _____ = _____

② There are 7 apples in a bag and m baskets of apples with 12 apples in each basket. How many apples are there?

   a. Number of apples = _____

   b. If there are 5 baskets, how many apples are there?
      Number of apples = _____ = _____

③ Tony has $3. p of his friends have $5 each. How much money do they have altogether?

   a. Altogether they have : $(_____)

   b. If there are 8 friends, how much money do they and Tony have altogether?
      Altogether they have : $(_____) = $_____

BEDMAS$

Evaluate each expression when n = 12.

④ $3n - 9$ =	⑤ $6 + 7n$ =
⑥ $n \div 3 + 12$ =	⑦ $81 - n \div 2$ =

Evaluate each expression when x = 3 and y = 16.

⑧ $2x + y$ = __22__   2(3)+16

⑨ $3y - 4x$ = ____   3(16) - 4(3)
                       48 - 12

⑩ $y \div 4 + 2x$ = __10__   16÷4+2(3)

⑪ $3x - y \div 8$ = __7__

⑫ $y - 2x + 6$ = __16__   16-2(3)+6 = 6

⑬ $y \div 2 + x \div 3$ = ____

> Substitute the numbers for the unknowns, but remember the order of operation.

Follow Tony's method to solve the equations.

Addition equation
$x + 8 = 15$
$x + 8 - 8 = 15 - 8$
$x = 7$ ↑ Subtract 8 from both sides.

Subtraction equation
$y - 6 = 10$
$y - 6 + 6 = 10 + 6$
$y = 16$ ↑ Add 6 to both sides.

> To solve an addition equation, subtract the same number from both sides of the equation.

> To solve a subtraction equation, add the same number to both sides of the equation.

⑭ $k + 5 = 19$ k = __14__

⑮ $p - 0.7 = 8$ p = ____

⑯ $v + 2.4 = 6$ v = ____

⑰ $u + 1.3 = 2.1$ u = ____

⑱ $9.8 + a = 10.2$ a = ____

⑲ $p - 4 = 2.3$ p = ____

⑳ $1.1 + m = 1.1$ m = ____

㉑ $n - 0.8 = 0.8$ n = ____

㉒ $z - 32 = 4$ z = ____

㉓ $b - 3 = \dfrac{1}{2}$ b = ____

㉔ $q - \dfrac{1}{2} = \dfrac{1}{4}$ q = ____

㉕ $r + \dfrac{1}{5} = \dfrac{3}{5}$ r = ____

Follow Helen's method to solve the equations.

Multiplication equation

$3y = 18$
$3y \div 3 = 18 \div 3$
$y = 6$

Divide both sides by 3.

Division equation

$x \div 6 = 2$
$x \div 6 \times 6 = 2 \times 6$
$x = 12$

Multiply both sides by 6.

To solve a multiplication equation, divide both sides of the equation by the same number.

Tip 7

㉖ $4n = 40$ $n = \underline{10}$

㉗ $0.2a = 3$ $a = \underline{}$

㉘ $\dfrac{1}{2}q = 11$ $q = \underline{}$ ㉙ $p \div 0.4 = 2$ $p = \underline{}$

㉚ $\dfrac{v}{5} = 0.2$ $v = \underline{}$ ㉛ $z \div 7 = 0.5$ $z = \underline{}$

㉜ $0.9s = 0$ $s = \underline{}$ ㉝ $0.8u = 0.2$ $u = \underline{}$

㉞ $\dfrac{b}{5} = 5$ $b = \underline{}$ ㉟ $t \div 1.2 = 1$ $t = \underline{}$

Find the ordered pairs and draw the graphs. Then use the graphs to find the values of y.

When $x = 1$, then $y = 1 + 1 = 2$.

$y = x + 1$

x	y	(x, y)
1	2	(1, 2)
2	3	(2, 3)
4	5	(4, 5)

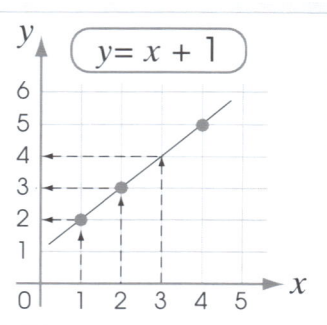

㊱ a.

$y = x + 2$

x	y	(x, y)
0		
2		
3		

b.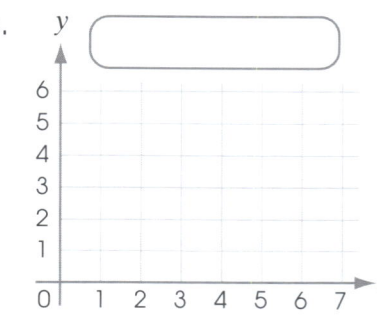

c. When $x = 1$,

$y = \underline{}$.

37. a.

$y = x - 1$		
x	y	(x, y)
1	0	(1, 0)
3	2	(3, 2)
5	4	(5, 4)

b.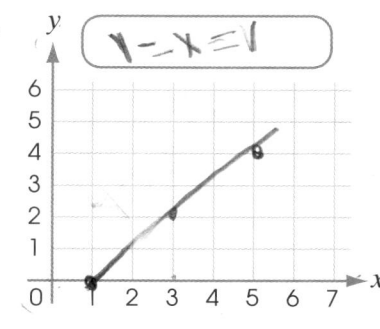

$y = x - 1$

c. When $x = 4$,

$y = $ __3__.

$Y = X - 1$
$y = 4 - 1$
$y = 3$

38. a.

$y = 6 - x$		
x	y	(x, y)
0		
2		
4		

b.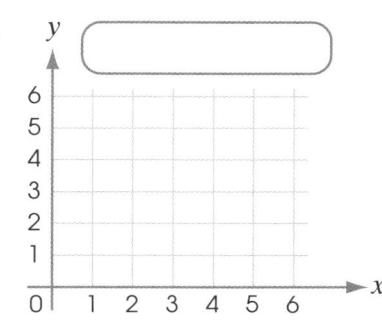

c. When $x = 3$,

$y = $ _____.

39. a.

$y = x \div 2$		
x	y	(x, y)
2		
4		
6		

b.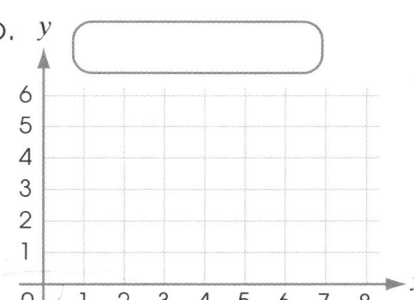

c. When $x = 8$,

$y = $ _____.

ACTIVITY

Read the graph and do the questions.

1. Complete the table.

Time (h)	Distance (km)	(Time , Distance)
1		
2		
4		
6		

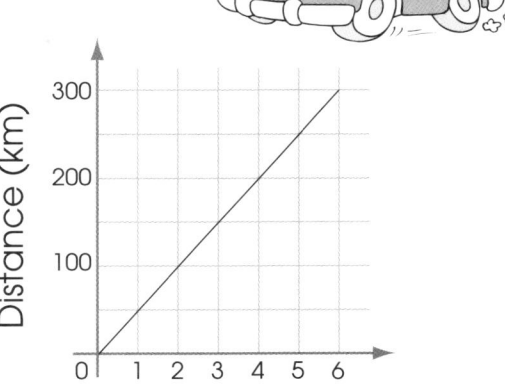

2. Circle the correct equation.

$y = 50 + x$ $y = 50x$ $x = 50y$

3 Fractions

WORDS TO LEARN

Reciprocal — either of a pair of numbers whose product is 1

e.g. $\dfrac{4}{3}$ is the reciprocal of $\dfrac{3}{4}$.

Follow Dave's method to find each product. Write the answers in simplest form.

$$3\dfrac{1}{3} \times 2\dfrac{1}{4} = \dfrac{\overset{5}{\cancel{10}}}{\cancel{3}_1} \times \dfrac{\overset{3}{\cancel{9}}}{\cancel{4}_2}$$

$$= \dfrac{5 \times 3}{2}$$

$$= \dfrac{15}{2} = 7\dfrac{1}{2}$$

- **1st** Change the mixed numbers to improper fractions.
- **2nd** Simplify by the common factors.
- **3rd** Multiply.
- **4th** Write in simplest form.

① $2\dfrac{1}{3} \times 1\dfrac{1}{2} =$

② $5\dfrac{1}{2} \times \dfrac{4}{11} =$

③ $2\dfrac{5}{6} \times 7\dfrac{1}{2} =$

④ $4 \times 3\dfrac{5}{8} =$

⑤ $3\dfrac{3}{7} \times 14 =$

⑥ $7\dfrac{1}{3} \times 4\dfrac{1}{2} =$

Tip **8**

Solve the problems.

⑦ $\dfrac{3}{4}$ of 40 students went climbing. How many students went climbing?

_____ students

⑧ Tony climbed $3\dfrac{1}{2}$ m/min. How far could he climb in $2\dfrac{1}{4}$ min?

_____ m

⑨ Tony brought 2L of water with him. He drank $\dfrac{7}{8}$ of it. How much did he drink?

_____ L

Follow Elaine's method to do the division. Write the answers in simplest form.

$$2\tfrac{1}{2} \div 1\tfrac{1}{2} = \tfrac{5}{2} \div \tfrac{3}{2}$$
$$= \tfrac{5}{2} \times \tfrac{2}{3}$$
$$= \tfrac{5}{3}$$
$$= 1\tfrac{2}{3}$$

- **1st** Change the mixed numbers to improper fractions.
- **2nd** Change the divisor to its reciprocal and ÷ to ×.
- **3rd** Simplify by the common factors.
- **4th** Multiply.
- **5th** Write in simplest form.

⑩ $\dfrac{2}{3} \div \dfrac{1}{15} =$ ⑪ $3\dfrac{1}{3} \div \dfrac{5}{6} =$

⑫ $\dfrac{3}{4} \div 4\dfrac{1}{2} =$ ⑬ $8 \div 3\dfrac{2}{3} =$

⑭ $6\dfrac{1}{4} \div 1\dfrac{1}{2} =$ ⑮ $2\dfrac{1}{5} \div \dfrac{1}{10} =$

⑯ $5\dfrac{5}{6} \div 15 =$ ⑰ $5 \div 2\dfrac{1}{7} =$

Tip 9

Solve the problems.

⑱ Tony shared $2\dfrac{1}{2}$ L of water with 3 friends. How much did each get? _____ L

⑲ Helen cut a $11\dfrac{1}{4}$ m rope into 3 equal pieces. How long was each piece? _____ m

⑳ Dave climbed $5\dfrac{1}{2}$ m in $1\dfrac{3}{8}$ min. What was his average speed? _____ m/min

Solve the problems. Then write the letters to find what Tony says.

㉑ $(\frac{1}{5} + \frac{2}{5}) \times \frac{5}{7} =$ ☐ i

㉒ $\frac{5}{6} \div (\frac{1}{12} + \frac{5}{12}) =$ ☐ e

㉓ $(\frac{3}{10} + \frac{9}{10}) \div \frac{4}{5} =$ ☐ g

㉔ $8 \div \frac{4}{7} \times \frac{1}{2} =$ ☐ m

㉕ $(\frac{1}{4} + 1\frac{1}{2}) \times \frac{1}{14} =$ ☐ c

㉖ $(4 - 2\frac{1}{3}) \times \frac{3}{7} =$ ☐ a

㉗ $\frac{2}{3} \times (\frac{9}{16} - \frac{1}{16}) =$ ☐ n

㉘ $(1\frac{1}{5} - \frac{1}{2}) \div \frac{7}{8} =$ ☐ i

㉙ $\frac{3}{4} \div (1\frac{1}{2} - \frac{1}{8}) =$ ☐ l

㉚ $\frac{3}{5} \div 2\frac{1}{5} \times 22 =$ ☐ b

㉛ I like $\frac{1}{8}$ $\frac{6}{11}$ $\frac{3}{7}$ 7 6 $\frac{4}{5}$ $\frac{1}{3}$ $1\frac{1}{2}$ very much.

Solve the problems.

㉜ Elaine climbed $3\frac{1}{3}$ m in 1 min. How long did she take to climb $7\frac{1}{2}$ m?

_____

She took _____ min.

㉝ The temperature dropped by $1\frac{1}{5}$ °C every hour. How many °C did it drop in $3\frac{1}{3}$ hours?

_____

It dropped _____ °C.

㉞ Helen spilt $\frac{2}{3}$ of a $2\frac{1}{2}$ L bottle of water. How much water did she spill?

_____

She spilt _____ L of water.

㉟ Dave shared $\frac{3}{4}$ kg of jelly beans with 3 friends. How many grams of beans did each get?

_____

Each got _____ grams of jelly beans.

㊱ A bottle of water was $\frac{7}{8}$ full. Tony drank $\frac{2}{5}$ of it. How much water was left?

_____

_____ of a bottle of water was left.

ACTIVITY

Write the answers as fractions in simplest form.

1.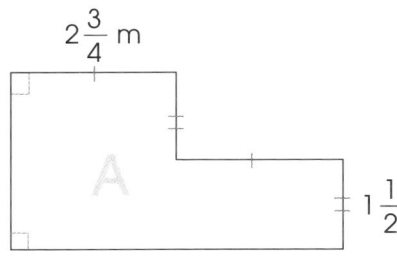

   $2\frac{3}{4}$ m, $1\frac{1}{2}$ m

   Area = _____ m²

2.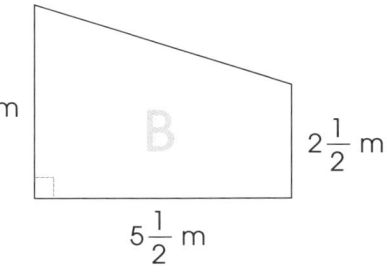

   $4\frac{1}{4}$ m, $2\frac{1}{2}$ m, $5\frac{1}{2}$ m

   Area = _____ m²

3. How many times is Shape B bigger than Shape A? _____ times

4 Percent

WORDS TO LEARN

Discount - the difference between the regular price and the sale price of an item
Sales tax - money paid to the government on things we buy

Express each fraction as a percent. Round to the nearest hundredth, if necessary.

$$\frac{4}{5} = \frac{4}{5} \times 100\% \overset{20}{\underset{1}{}}$$
$$= 80\%$$

$$1\frac{1}{4} = \frac{5}{4} \times 100\% \overset{25}{\underset{1}{}}$$
$$= 125\%$$

Tip 10

① $\frac{9}{25}$ = ☐   ② $\frac{5}{8}$ = ☐

③ $\frac{3}{7}$ = ☐   ④ $\frac{11}{16}$ = ☐

⑤ $1\frac{4}{5}$ = ☐   ⑥ $2\frac{6}{7}$ = ☐   ⑦ $1\frac{4}{15}$ = ☐

Express each percent as a fraction in simplest form.

⑧ 50% = $\frac{1}{2}$ ⑨ 46% = $\frac{12}{25}$ ⑩ 24% = $\frac{6}{25}$

⑪ 8% = $\frac{2}{25}$ ⑫ 2% = $\frac{1}{50}$ ⑬ 78% = $\frac{39}{50}$

Find the percent of the shaded parts in each shape. Round to the nearest hundredth, if necessary.

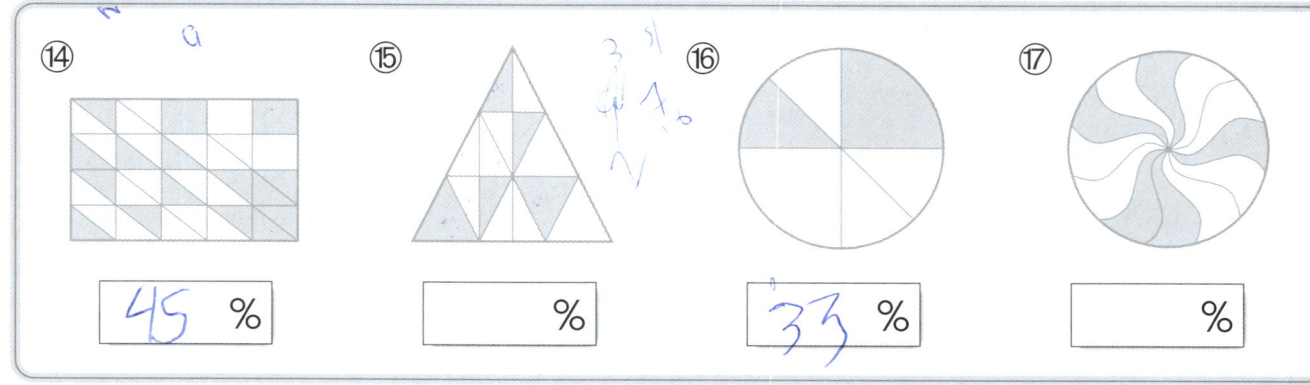

⑭ 45 %   ⑮ ___ %   ⑯ 33 %   ⑰ ___ %

Follow Tony's method to solve the problems.

30.5% of 400 T-shirts are on sale. How many T-shirts are on sale?

$$400 \times 30.5\% = \overset{4}{400} \times \frac{30.5}{\underset{1}{100}} = 122$$

122 T-shirts are on sale.

⑱ 15% of 250 = _____   ⑲ 16% of 210 = _____

⑳ 32.5% of 500 = _____   ㉑ 18.7% of 400 = _____

㉒ 64% of 37.5 = _____   ㉓ 25% of 64.8 = _____

㉔ There are 120 skirts in the store. 15% of them are blue, 20% red and the rest black.

   a. How many blue skirts are there? __18__ blue skirts

   b. How many red skirts are there? __24__ red skirts

   c. How many black skirts are there? __42__ black skirts

Read what Dave says. Then help him solve the problems.

90 out of 120 customers in the store are women. What percent of the customers are women?

$$\frac{90}{120} \times 100\% = 75\%$$

㉕ 35 out of 350 _____ %   ㉖ 75 out of 250 _____ %

㉗ $7\frac{1}{2}$ out of 200 _____ %   ㉘ 6 out of 120 _____ %

㉙ 65 out of 250 people in the store have bought something. How many percent of the people have bought things in the store?

_____ % of the people have bought things in the store.

See how Tony finds the sale price of the cap. Then help him find the sale prices of the other items. Round to the nearest hundredth, if necessary.

Reg. $15
20% Off
Sale $ 12

Since 100% − 20% = 80%, the sale price is 80% of the regular price.

80% of $15 = 0.8 × $15
= $12

The sale price of  is $12.

㉚ Reg. $41.50
15% Off
Sale $ _____

㉛ Reg. $82.75
25% Off
Sale $ _____

㉜ Reg. $23.90
40% Off
Sale $ _____

㉝ Reg. $69.99
10% Off
Sale $ _____

㉞ Reg. $32.90
35% Off
Sale $ _____

㉟ Reg. $34.50
30% Off
Sale $ _____

The tax rate is 15%. Help Tony find the total cost of each item. Round to the nearest hundredth, if necessary.

㊱  $56
Total cost
$ _____

㊲  $22.99
Total cost
$ _____

$49

Tax:
$49 × 15%
= $7.35

Total cost:
$49 + $7.35
= $56.35

㊳ $42.59
Total cost
$ _____

㊴ $38.29
Total cost
$ _____

Read what the children say. Then complete the tables.

	Regular Price	Discount Rate	Amount of Discount	Sale Price
	$20	40%	$8	$12
㊵	$90			$58.50
㊶			$11.25	$63.75
㊷	$35.85		$7.17	

I have saved $8 out of $20.

Discount rate
$= \frac{8}{20} \times 100\%$
$= 40\%$

	Selling Price	Tax Rate	Amount of Tax	Total Cost
	$16	15%	$2.40	$18.40
㊸	$40		$2.80	
㊹			$3.54	$33.04
㊺	$82.50			$87.45

Tax rate
$= \frac{2.4}{16} \times 100\%$
$= 15\%$

Solve the problems. Round the answers to the nearest hundredth, if necessary.

㊻ All items in a shop are 25% off. What is the sale price of a $36 helmet if there is an additional 15% off the reduced price?

$ _____

㊼ Helen bought a $46.59 skirt at 30% off. How much did she pay with a tax rate of 9%?

$ _____

㊽ Tony bought a shirt for $22.50 and bought a second one at a discount of 50%. How much did he pay for the two shirts with a tax rate of 7%?

$ _____

ACTIVITY

The dimensions of Uncle Fred's shop are 18m by 10m, but it will be 10% longer and 10% wider after the renovations. How much bigger will Uncle Fred's shop be after the renovations?

His shop will be _____ m² bigger.

5 Measurement

WORDS TO LEARN

Perimeter - the distance around the outside of a shape
Area - the number of square units of a surface
Volume - the number of cubic units occupied by an object

Help Tony find the perimeter and area of each shape.

①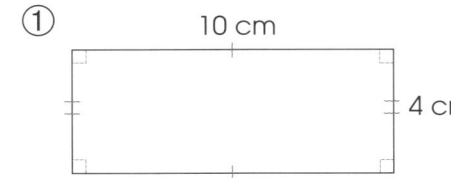

Perimeter = _____ cm
Area = _____ cm²

② 4.5 m square

Perimeter = _____ m
Area = _____ m²

③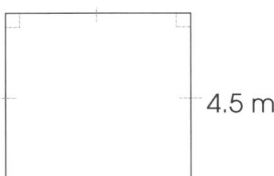

Perimeter = _____ cm
Area = _____ cm²

l = length
b = width

Area of rectangle
= length x width
= $l \times b$

④ 3.2 m, 1.1 m, 3.6 m (parallelogram)

Perimeter = _____ m
Area = _____ m²

⑤ 4 cm, 3 cm, 4.5 cm, 5 cm, 8 cm

Perimeter = _____ cm
Area = _____ cm²

Tip **11**

Tip **12**

⑥ 6.5 m, 1.2 m, 5.5 m, 3.2 m, 4.5 m

Perimeter = _____ m
Area = _____ m²

18 MATHSMART (GRADE 7)

Follow Tony's method to find the area of each trapezoid.

Two congruent trapezoids
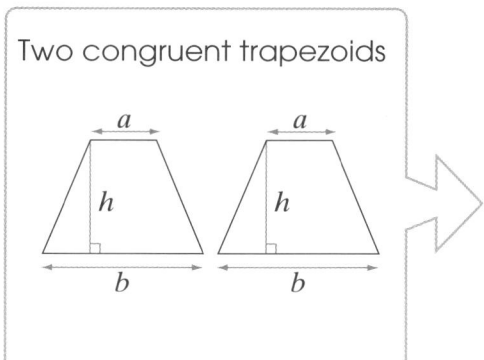

Put them together to form a parallelogram.
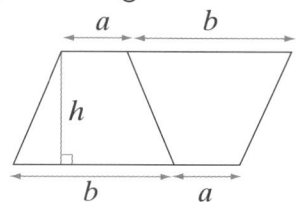

Area of this parallelogram = $(a+b)h$

The area of a trapezoid is one half the product of its height and the sum of its bases.

⑦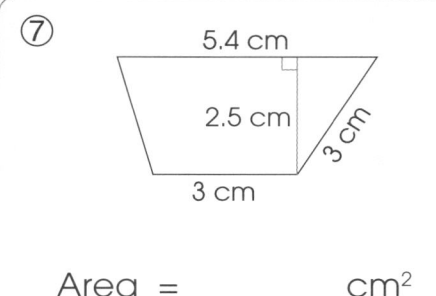

Area = _____ cm²

⑧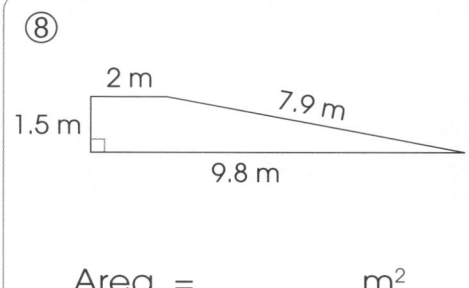

Area = _____ m²

Tip 13

⑨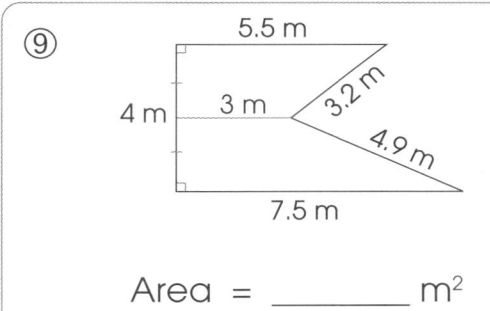

Area = _____ m²

⑩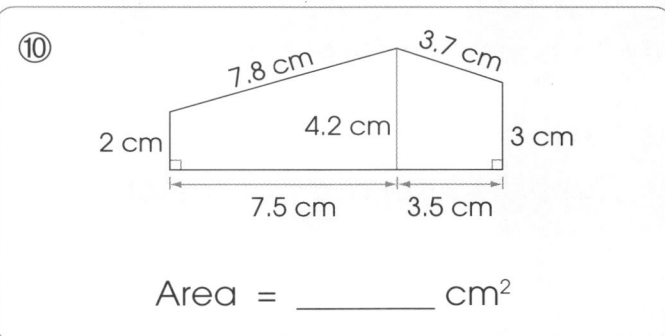

Area = _____ cm²

Find the area of the shaded parts.

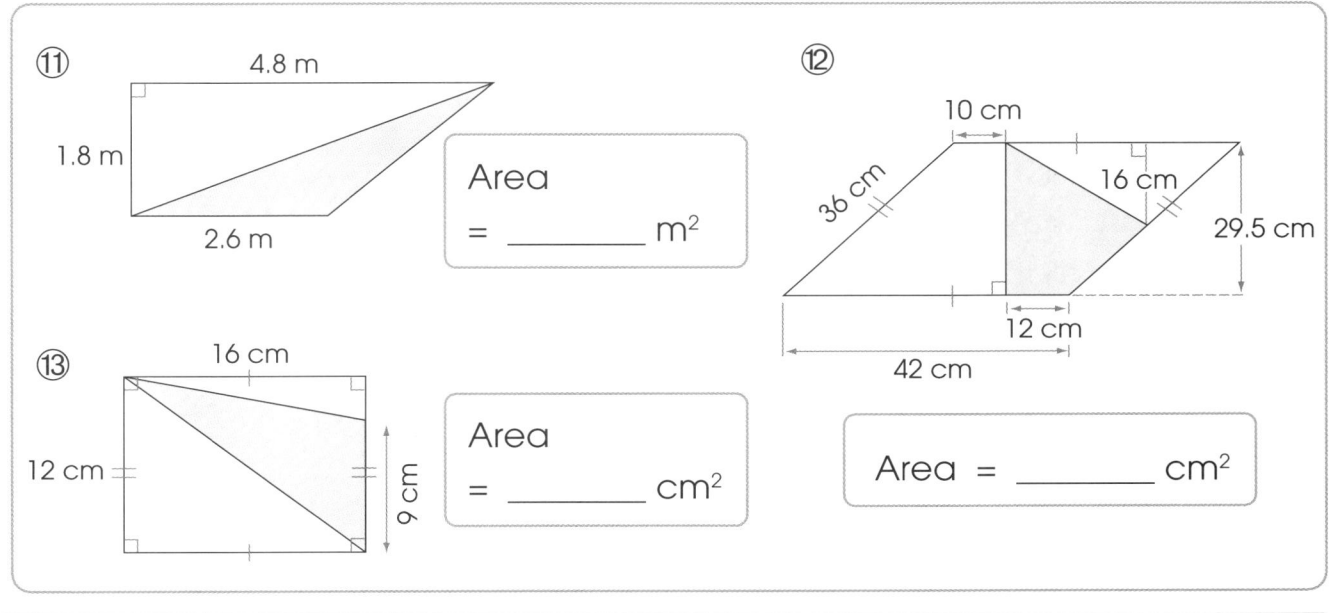

⑪ Area = _____ m²

⑫ Area = _____ cm²

⑬ Area = _____ cm²

Fill in the blanks.

⑭ 14 m² = _____ cm²

⑮ 16.5 m² = _____ cm²

⑯ 8.45 m² = _____ cm²

⑰ 940 m² = _____ cm²

Tip 14

Tip 15

⑱ 1 260 000 cm² = _____ m²   ⑲ 47 320 cm² = _____ m²

Help Tony solve the problems.

⑳ Tony's bedroom is 4 m long and 3.8 m wide. Carpeting the floor costs $49 per m². How much will it cost to carpet the entire floor?

It costs $_____ to carpet the entire floor.

㉑ The walls of Tony's bedroom are 2.5 m high. Two of the walls are 4 m long and the other two 3.8 m long. If a can of paint can cover 24 m², how many cans of paint will Tony need to paint all the walls?

Tony needs _____ cans of paint to paint all the walls.

Tick ✔ the best units for measuring the volume of Tony's boxes.

㉒   ㉓

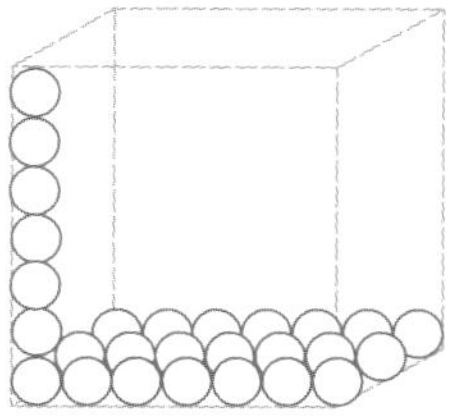

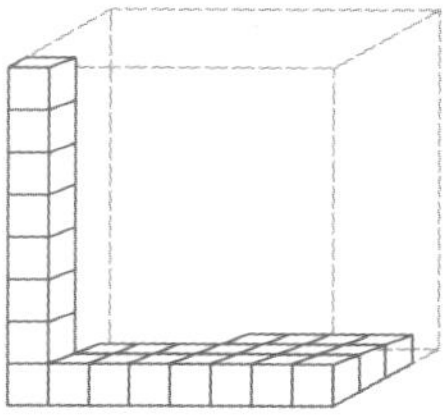

㉔   ㉕

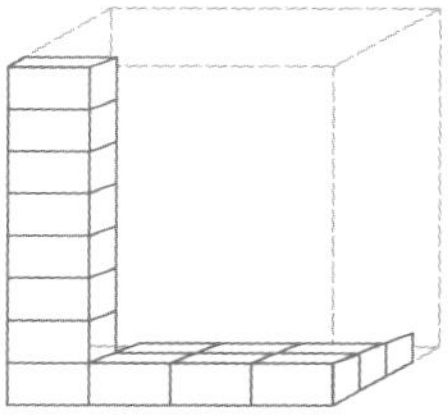

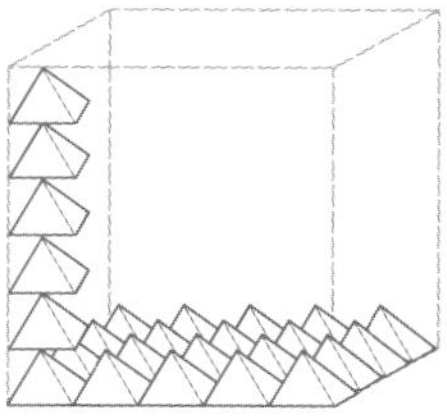

Help Tony find the volume of his blocks.

㉖ 4 cm, 2 cm, 3 cm
Volume = _____ cm³

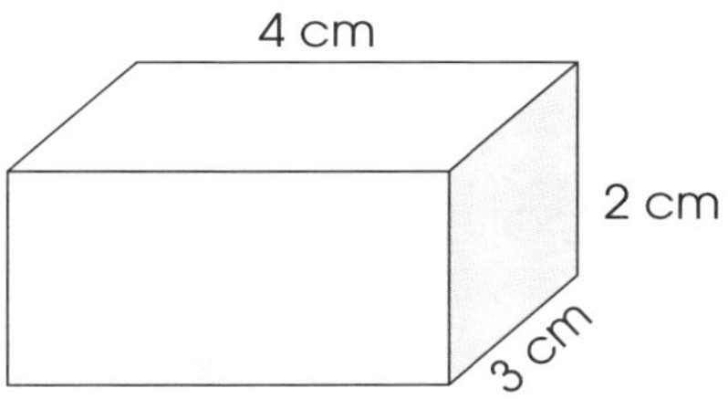

㉗ 8 cm, 6 cm, 7.5 cm
Volume = _____ cm³

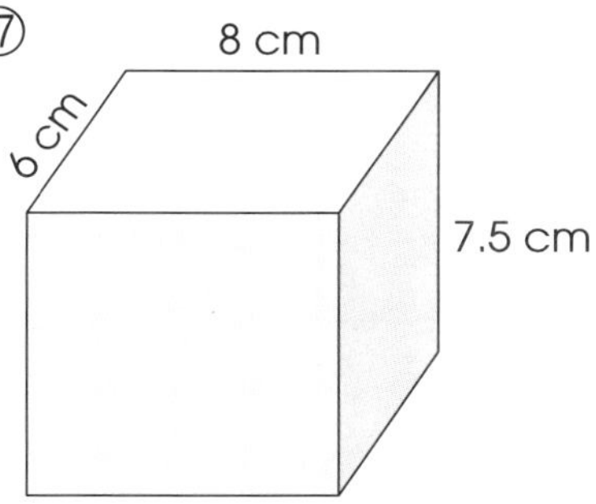

Tip 16

㉘ 13 cm, 5 cm, 1.5 cm
Volume = _____ cm³

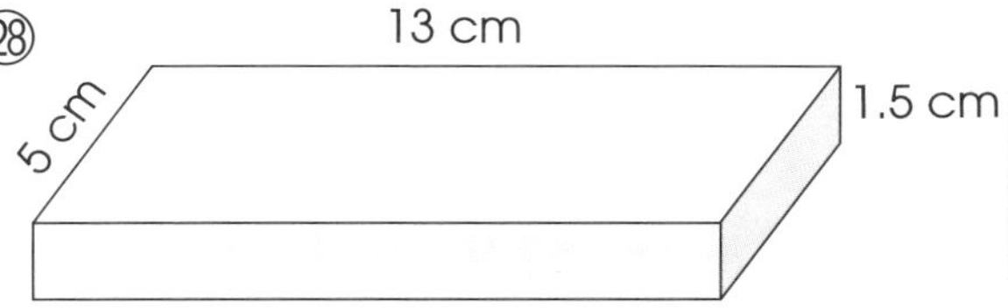

㉙ 5 cm, 3 cm, 4 cm, 6 cm, 12 cm
Volume = _____ cm³

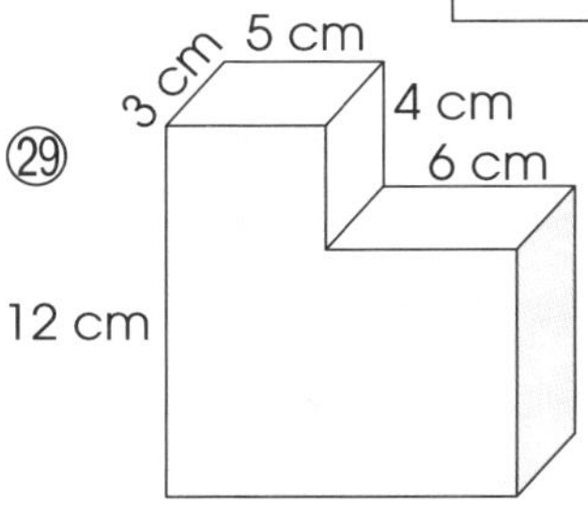

㉚ 3 cm, 2 cm, 4 cm, 9.5 cm, 16.8 cm
Volume = _____ cm³

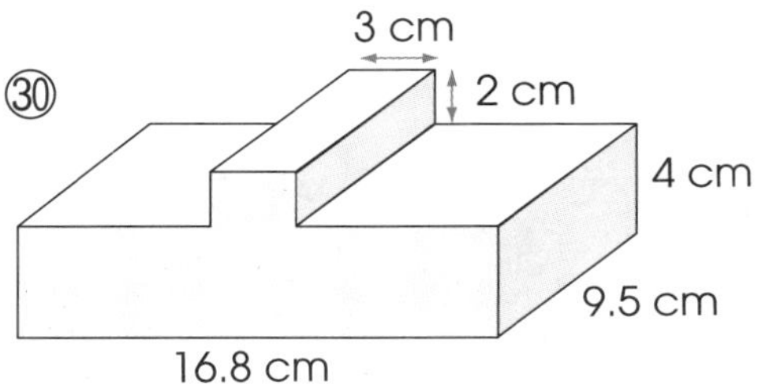

Help Tony find the area of the base and volume of each block.

㉛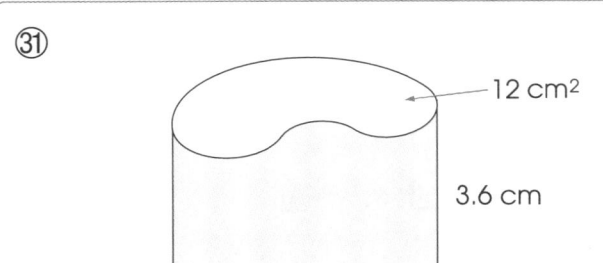

- 12 cm²
- 3.6 cm

Area of base = _____ cm²
Volume = _____ cm³

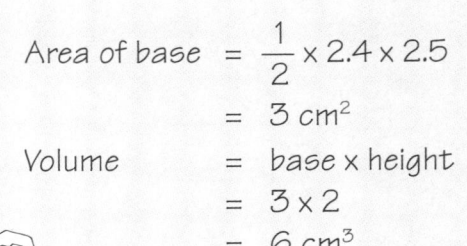

Area of base = $\frac{1}{2} \times 2.4 \times 2.5$
= 3 cm²
Volume = base × height
= 3 × 2
= 6 cm³

Tip 17

㉜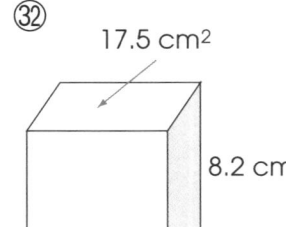
- 17.5 cm²
- 8.2 cm

Area of base = _____ cm²
Volume = _____ cm³

㉝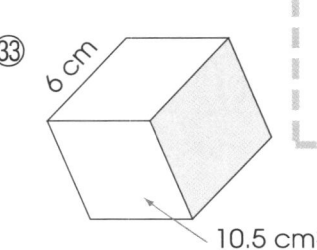
- 6 cm
- 10.5 cm²

Area of base = _____ cm²
Volume = _____ cm³

㉞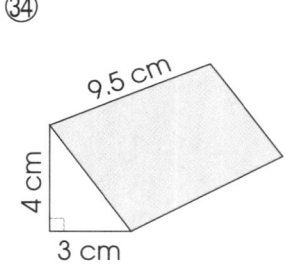
- 9.5 cm
- 4 cm
- 3 cm

Area of base = _____ cm²
Volume = _____ cm³

㉟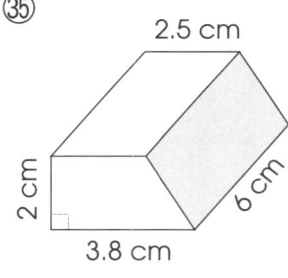
- 2.5 cm
- 2 cm
- 6 cm
- 3.8 cm

Area of base = _____ cm²
Volume = _____ cm³

㊱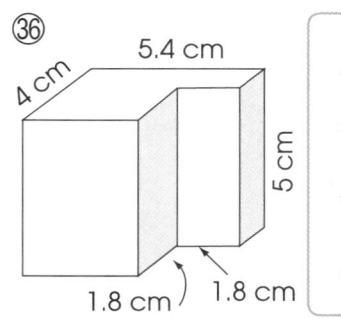
- 5.4 cm
- 4 cm
- 5 cm
- 1.8 cm
- 1.8 cm

Area of base = _____ cm²
Volume = _____ cm³

㊲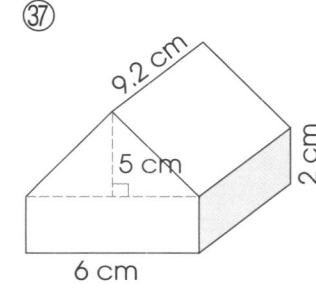
- 9.2 cm
- 5 cm
- 2 cm
- 6 cm

Area of base = _____ cm²
Volume = _____ cm³

Fill in the blanks.

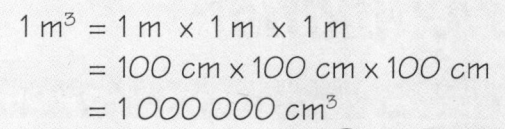

㊳ 2 356 000 cm³ = _____ m³

㊴ 1 730 000 cm³ = _____ m³

㊵ 360 000 cm³ = _____ m³

㊶ 1.5 m³ = _____ cm³

㊷ 0.007 m³ = _____ cm³

㊸ 0.6 m³ = _____ cm³

㊹ 1.04 m³ = _____ cm³

Solve the problems.

㊺ A rectangular box is 1 m long, 30 cm wide and 40 cm high. What is the volume of the box in cm³ and in m³?

_____ cm³ , _____ m³

㊻ What is the height of solid A if its volume is equal to the volume of solid B?

_____ cm

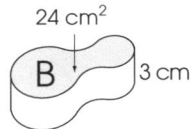

ACTIVITY

Use the following method to find the area of each polygon.

m = no. of • on the perimeter of the polygon
n = no. of • inside the polygon
A = area of the polygon

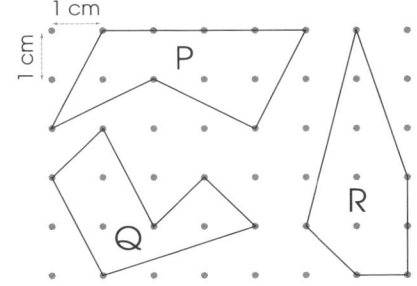

Polygon	m	n	A = 0.5 m − 1 + n
P	8	3	0.5 × 8 − 1 + 3 = 6 cm²
1. Q			cm²
2. R			cm²

MathSmart (Grade 7) 23

6 Approximation

WORDS TO LEARN

Approximate - nearly correct but not exact
≈ - approximation sign

Tell which of the following show an exact value or an approximate value. Write E for exact and A for approximate.

① The weight of the book is about 1.2 kg. ☐

② The book has 290 pages. ☐

③ The book is about 2.8 cm thick. ☐

④ The cost of the book is $17.25. ☐

⑤ The area of the book is about 602 cm^2. ☐

Follow Tony's method to find the approximation for the area of each shape.

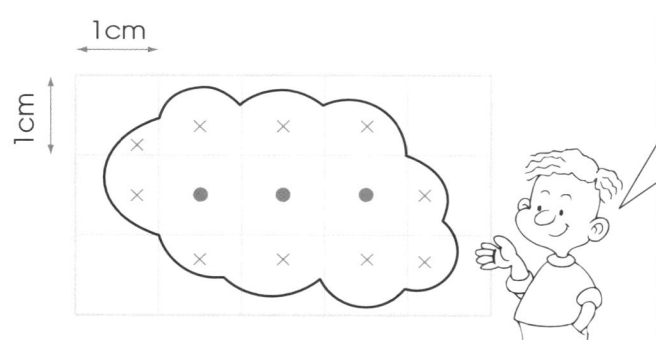

Number of full squares = 3
Area = 3 cm^2

Number of partly shaded squares = 10
Area ≈ 10 × 0.5   approximates to
≈ 5 cm^2

Area of this shape ≈ 8 cm^2

⑥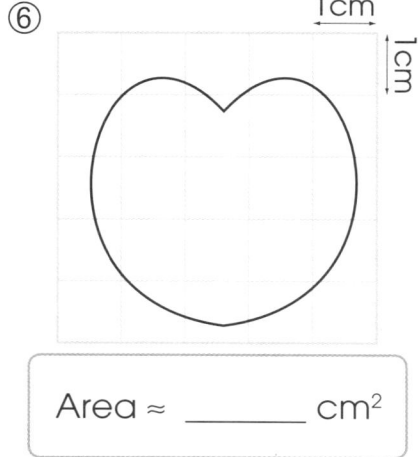

Area ≈ _____ cm^2

⑦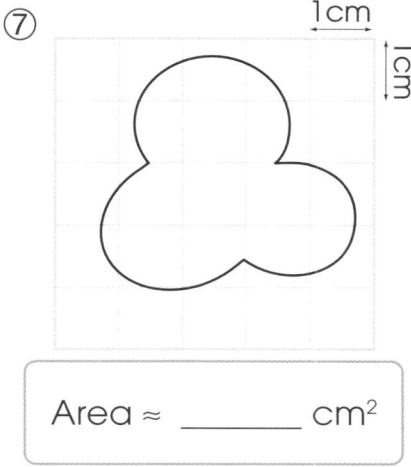

Area ≈ _____ cm^2

Tip 20

⑧ Area ≈ _____ cm²

⑨ Area ≈ _____ cm²

Help Dave complete the table.

The length of AB to the nearest cm : AB ≈ 5 cm

The length of AB to the nearest 0.5 cm : AB ≈ 4.5 cm

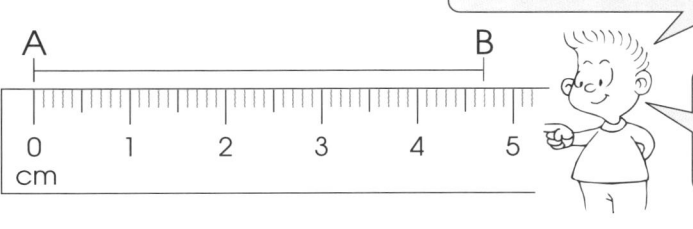

Line	Length to the nearest cm	Length to the nearest 0.5 cm
⑩ MN		
⑪ PQ		
⑫ RS		
⑬ MS		

ACTIVITY

Estimate the number of marbles that can be put into the box. Then find the exact number.

Diameter 1 cm

Estimate : ____

Exact : ____

7 Integers

WORDS TO LEARN

Number line - a straight line on which numbers are represented by intervals marked to scale eg. number line −1 0 1 2

Opposites - the two numbers that are the same distance from zero but in opposite directions on the number line eg. −5 and 5 are opposites.

Integers - whole numbers and their opposites and zero   eg. 20, −5, 0, 4, ...

Follow Dave's method to write the number as integers.

The temperature is 20 °C above 0 °C. ⇒ + 20 °C.

The temperature is 15 °C below 0 °C. ⇒ −15 °C.

① The profit of a company:

    a. gain $1200   b. loss $450

② Tony's weight:

    a. increased by 1 kg   b. decreased by 3 kg

Put < or >.

③ −3 ___ 0   ④ −4 ___ −1   ⑤ −9 ___ −6

⑥ −5 ___ −8   ⑦ +2 ___ −4   ⑧ +3 ___ +8

Write in order from the least to the greatest.

⑨ −3, −6, 0, +4, +2 _____

⑩ +5, −4, −3, +7, +1 _____

⑪ −1, 0, +6, −5, +3 _____

Tip 21

Tip 22

MathSmart (Grade 7)

Follow Dave's method to write an addition sentence for each diagram.

(+2) + (+3) = +5

(+2) + (−4) = −2

(−1) + (−4) = −5

(−2) + (+3) = +1

⑫ ( ) + ( ) = _____

⑬ ( ) + ( ) = _____

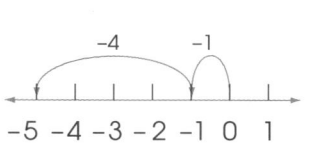

⑭ ( ) + ( ) = _____

⑮ ( ) + ( ) = _____

⑯ ( ) + ( ) = _____

Do the addition.

⑰ (−5) + (−7) = _____

⑱ (+2) + (−7) = _____

⑲ (−2) + (−1) = _____

⑳ (+6) + (+6) = _____

㉑ (−4) + (+4) = _____

㉒ (−8) + (+4) = _____

㉓ (+8) + (+1) + (+2) = _____

㉔ (+3) + (−7) + (−1) = _____

㉕ (+3) + (−8) + (−2) = _____

㉖ (−2) + (+3) + (+3) = _____

㉗ (+1) + (+9) + (−2) = _____

㉘ (−3) + (−2) + (−1) = _____

MATHSMART (GRADE 7) 27

Follow Tony's method to write the opposite of each integer.

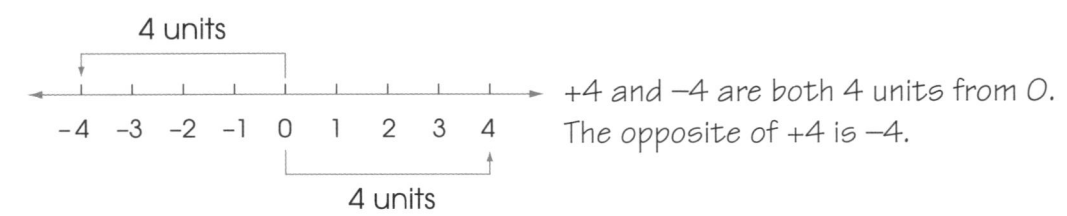 

㉙ +6 _____ ㉚ −7 _____ ㉛ +26 _____ ㉜ −20 _____

㉝ −3 _____ ㉞ +4 _____ ㉟ −9 _____ ㊱ +10 _____

Read what Helen says. Then do the subtraction.

To subtract an integer, we can add its opposite.

$$(-6) - (-5) = (-6) + (+5) \qquad (-3) - (+6) = -3 + (-6)$$
$$ = -1 \qquad\qquad\qquad = -9$$

㊲ (−5) − (−4) = ( ) + ( )   ㊳ (+4) − (+7) = ( ) + ( )
= _____   = _____

㊴ (−13) − (+2) = ( ) + ( )   ㊵ (+6) − (−10) = ( ) + ( )
= _____   = _____

Try these.

㊶ (−2) − (−4) = _____   ㊷ (+9) − (−2) = _____

㊸ (0) − (−8) = _____   ㊹ (+11) − (−11) = _____

㊺ (+4) − (+9) = _____   ㊻ (−7) − (−3) = _____

㊼ (+10) − (+4) − (−1) = _____   ㊽ (−6) − (+5) − (−3) = _____

㊾ (−5) − (−6) − (+4) = _____   ㊿ (+3) − (−7) − (+9) = _____

Read Tony's note and solve the problems. Then write the letters to find what Tony says.

Multiplying Integers

- When the signs of the factors are the same, the product is positive.

  e.g. $(+2) \times (+3) = +6$

  $(-2) \times (-3) = +6$

- When the signs of the factors are different, the product is negative.

  e.g. $(-2) \times (+3) = -6$

Dividing Integers

- When the signs are the same, the quotient is positive.

  e.g. $(+10) \div (+2) = +5$

  $(-10) \div (-2) = +5$

- When the signs are different, the quotient is negative.

  e.g. $(-10) \div (+5) = -2$

  $(+10) \div (-5) = -2$

(51) $(-11) \times (-2) =$ ____ s

(52) $(-6) \times (+9) =$ ____ k

(53) $(+5) \times (-6) =$ ____ i

(54) $(+10) \div (-2) =$ ____ c

(55) $(-4) \times (-5) =$ ____ r

(56) $(+20) \div (+4) =$ ____ o

(57) $(+21) \div (-3) =$ ____ e

(58) $(-18) \div (-6) =$ ____ t

(59) $(-7) \times (+5) =$ ____ a

(60) $(-4) \times (+5) =$ ____ f

(61) P [+20] [-35] [-5] [+3] [-30] [-5] [-7] m [-35] [-54] [-7] [+22] p [-7] [+20] [-20] [-7] [-5] [+3] .

ACTIVITY

Answer the questions.

	SUN	MON	TUE	WED	THU	FRI	SAT
Temp. (°C)	5	1	−6	−5	−2	2	4

1. Which day is the warmest? ____________

2. Which day is the coldest? ____________

3. What is the difference in temperature between Wednesday and Saturday? ____________ °C

Fractions, Decimals and Percent

WORDS TO LEARN

Formula - a general rule showing how variables are related to one another

Follow the children's method to complete the table. Round the answers to the nearest hundredth, if necessary.

$$\frac{3}{4} = \frac{3}{4} \times 100\% = 75\%$$

$$0.05 = 0.05 \times 100\% = 5\%$$

	Percent	Decimal	Fraction
①		0.2	
②	28%		
③			$\frac{9}{20}$
④		0.65	
⑤			$\frac{2}{3}$
⑥		1.4	
⑦			$2\frac{7}{10}$

Tip 25

Read what Tony says. Then help him solve the problems.

⑧ Tony ate 10% of 20 apples and Dave ate 12% of 25 apples. Who ate more apples? How many more?

10% of 20
= 10% × 20 = 0.1 × 20 = 2
I ate 2 apples.

_____ ate _____ more apple(s) than _____.

⑨ Helen spent 23.5% of $40 and Elaine spent $\frac{1}{8}$ of $74. Who spent more money? How much more?

_____ spent $_____ more than _____ .

⑩ Tony answered 84% of the 50 questions on the history test correctly. He answered 0.75 of the 60 questions on the math test correctly. On which test did he get more correct answers? How many more?

Tony got _____ more correct answers on the _____ test than on the _____ test.

Use the rules below to find the answers.

⑪ $(23 + 2) \div 5 + 6$ = _____

⑫ $24 \div (6 + 2) \times 5$ = _____

⑬ $(42 - 2) \div (4 + 6)$ = _____

⑭ $0.5 \times (18 + 2) \div \frac{1}{2}$ = _____

⑮ $(0.6 \times 10)^2 \div (11 + 1)$ = _____

⑯ $18 - (0.2 + 40\%) \times 8$ = _____

⑰ $0.9 + (4 + 2)^2 \div 2$ = _____

⑱ $0.5 \times (1.6 - 0.2) \div 4$ = _____

⑲ $650\% - (0.7 + 0.5)^2 \times 4 =$ _____

Order of Operations

1st Do all operations inside the brackets.

2nd Do exponents.

3rd Do multiplication and division from left to right.

4th Do addition and subtraction from left to right.

Tick ✔ the correct answers and grade the children's test papers.

⑳ *Dave White*   **MATH TEST**

1. $2^2 \times 0.3 - 1$ = 0.2 ✔
2. $(14 - \frac{1}{2} \times 10)^2$ = 81 ☐
3. $7 - 0.65 \times 10$ = 63.5 ☐
4. $18 - \frac{1}{4} \times 12 \div 2$ = 7.5 ☐
5. $30\% \times (15 - 9)^2$ = 10.8 ☐
6. $(12 - 2) \times 6 - 4^2$ = 44 ☐
7. $\frac{7}{12} \times 144 - 6 \div 3$ = 82 ☐
8. $10 - (35\% \times 9 - 2)$ = 8.85 ☐

GRADE: $\frac{\Box}{8}$ = $\Box$ %

㉑ *Steve Lindsay*   **MATH TEST**

1. $3^2 \times (15 - 12)$ = 27 ☐
2. $20 + 6 \times 3 \div 2$ = 29 ☐
3. $(4 + 5)^2 - 10 \times \frac{1}{2}$ = 76 ☐
4. $(40 - 26) \div 2 - 7$ = 0 ☐
5. $(0.2 + 50\%) \times 6^2$ = 25.2 ☐
6. $(0.5 + 5) \times 2^2$ = 121 ☐
7. $\frac{2}{5} \times 45 - 16 \times 80\%$ = 5.2 ☐
8. $(25 - 9) \div 4 + 50\% \times 6$ = 27 ☐

GRADE: $\frac{\Box}{8}$ = $\Box$ %

Use the given formulas to solve the problems. Round the answers to the nearest hundredth, if necessary.

㉒ Uncle Paul's wages:

   Wages = $500 + $10.5 × (number of working hours)

   a. If he works $4\frac{1}{2}$ hours, how much will he get? $_____

   b. If he works 8 hours, how much will he get? $_____

㉓ Taxi fare:

Taxi fare = $2.50 + $0.75 x (distance travelled in km)

a. If Tony travelled 8.7 km, how much would the fare be? $_____

b. If Tony travelled 10.25 km, how much would the fare be? $_____

㉔ The weight of a box of candies:

Weight = 400 g − 15 g x (number of candies eaten)

a. If Dave ate 5 candies, how heavy would the box be?   _____ g

b. If Dave ate 12 candies, how heavy would the box be?   _____ g

㉕ The money that Helen has:

Helen's money = (Dave's money + Steve's money) x 40%

a. If Dave has $25 and Steve has $35,
how much does Helen have? $_____

b. If Dave has $70.50 and Steve has $16,
how much does Helen have? $_____

ACTIVITY

Put brackets and operation signs to these numbers to produce the right answers.

$$2 \times (3 + 4) - 5 + 1 = 10$$

1. 5   2   4   3   1 = 10
2. 3   2   1   5   4 = 10
3. 5   2   1   4   3 = 10
4. ((4   2)   5)   3   1 = 10

Midway Test

Write each product as a power and state the base and exponent of each power.
(6 marks)

① $8 \times 8 \times 8 \times 8 \times 8 \times 8 \times 8 \times 8 \times 8 \times 8 \times 8 \times 8 =$ _____

Exponent = _____   Base = _____

② Four to the fifth power = _____

Exponent = _____   Base = _____

Find the prime factors of each number and write as a power. Then find the square root of each number. (8 marks)

③ 81 = _____
$\sqrt{81}$ = _____

④ 16 = _____
$\sqrt{16}$ = _____

⑤ 64 = _____
$\sqrt{64}$ = _____

⑥ 400 = ___ × ___
$\sqrt{400}$ = _____

⑦ 196 = ___ × ___
$\sqrt{196}$ = _____

⑧ 484 = ___ × ___
$\sqrt{484}$ = _____

Solve the equations. (8 marks)

⑨ $5 + y = 9$ $y =$ _____
⑩ $m - 7 = 14$ $m =$ _____

⑪ $p - 2.5 = 6.3$ $p =$ _____
⑫ $q + 1.4 = 2.7$ $q =$ _____

⑬ $0.2w = 5$ $w =$ _____
⑭ $t \div 6 = 0.9$ $t =$ _____

⑮ $\frac{1}{4}k = 0.3$ $k =$ _____
⑯ $z \div 0.5 = 4$ $z =$ _____

Write the answers in simplest form. (8 marks)

⑰ $2\frac{1}{3} \times \frac{4}{7} = $ _____

⑱ $5\frac{1}{6} \times 3 = $ _____

⑲ $1\frac{2}{5} \div \frac{7}{15} = $ _____

⑳ $2\frac{2}{5} \div 8 = $ _____

㉑ $\frac{2}{3} \times (\frac{2}{5} + \frac{4}{5}) = $ _____

㉒ $(\frac{1}{6} + 1\frac{1}{2}) \div \frac{5}{6} = $ _____

㉓ $\frac{5}{16} \div (2\frac{1}{8} - 1\frac{1}{2}) = $ _____

㉔ $\frac{4}{9} \times (2\frac{1}{12} - 1\frac{1}{3}) = $ _____

Solve the problems. (6 marks)

㉕ Each cup can hold $\frac{1}{6}$ L of juice. How many cups are needed for $1\frac{1}{3}$ L of juice? _____ cups

㉖ A mug can hold $\frac{7}{8}$ L of water. A glass can only hold $\frac{2}{3}$ as much. How much water can the glass hold? _____ L

㉗ A car travels $69\frac{1}{3}$ km an hour. How far can it travel in $1\frac{1}{2}$ hours? _____ km

Find the percent of the shaded parts in each shape. Round to the nearest hundredth, if necessary. (2 marks)

㉘  _____ %

㉙ 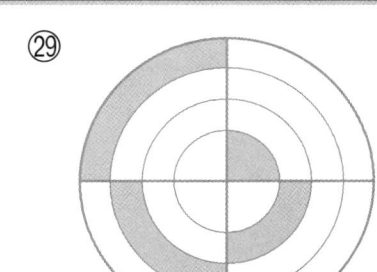 _____ %

Midway Test

Complete the tables. (14 marks)

	Regular Price	Discount Rate	Amount of Discount	Sale Price
㉚	$40	25%		
㉛	$75	30%		
㉜			$25.20	$100.80
㉝	$89.20		$13.38	

	Selling Price	Tax Rate	Amount of Tax	Total Cost
㉞	$36	12%		
㉟	$15.50		$1.24	
㊱			$11.34	$86.94

Find the perimeter and area of each shape. (8 marks)

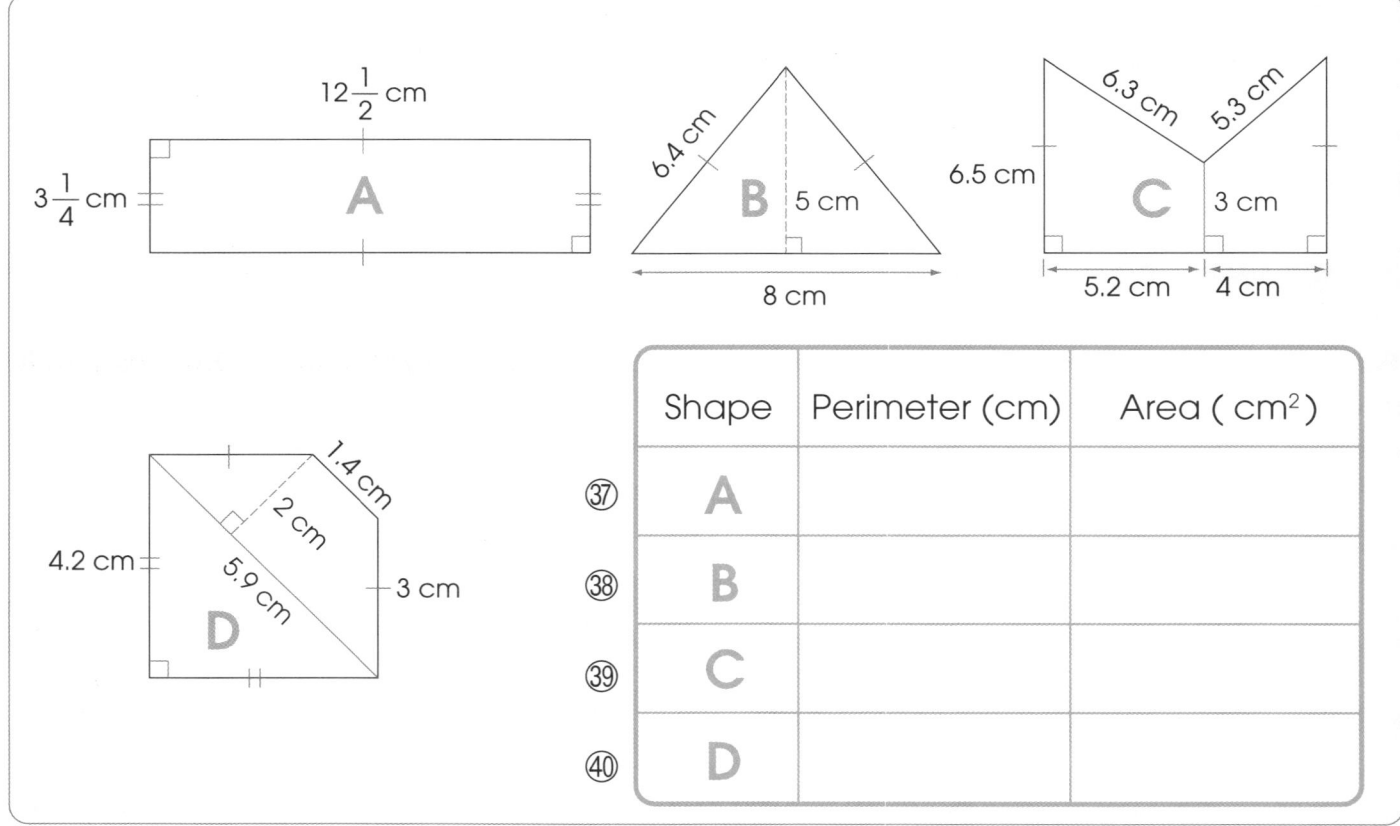

	Shape	Perimeter (cm)	Area (cm²)
㊲	A		
㊳	B		
㊴	C		
㊵	D		

Find the volume of each solid. (8 marks)

㊶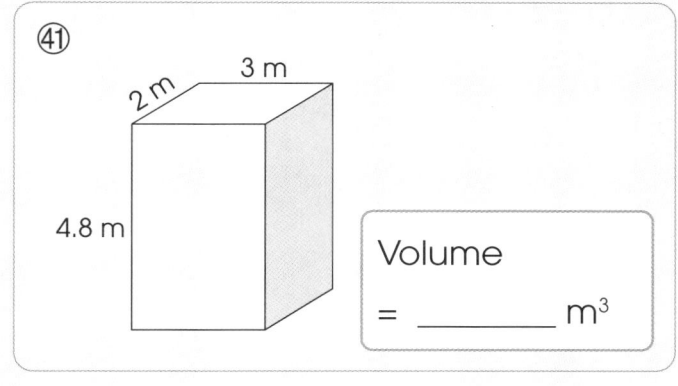

Volume = _____ m³

㊷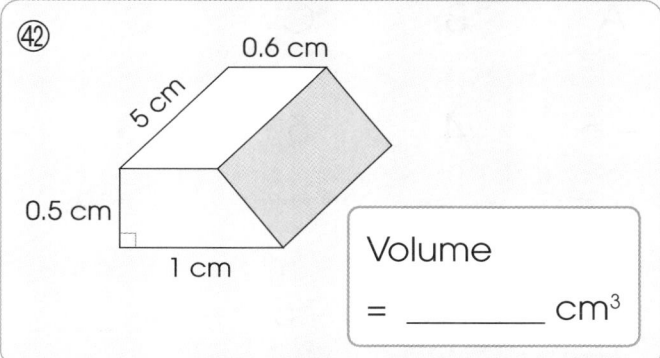

Volume = _____ cm³

㊸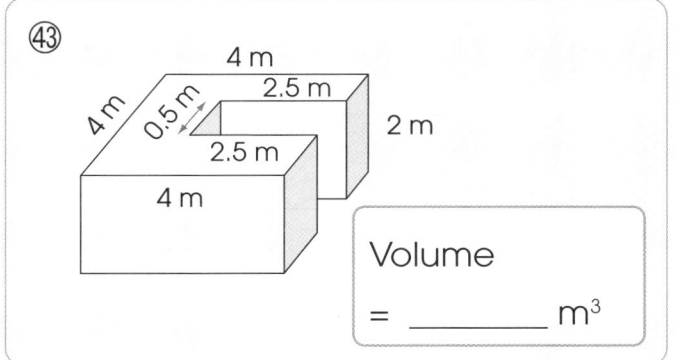

Volume = _____ m³

㊹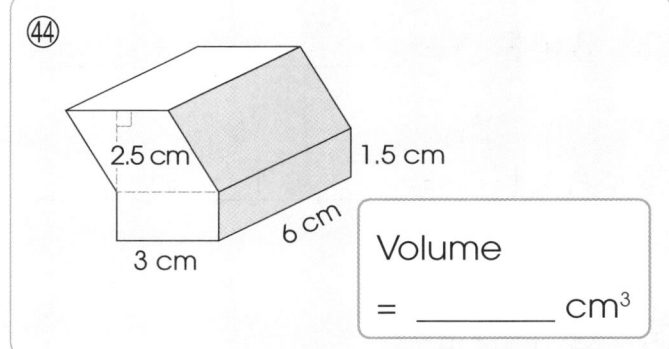

Volume = _____ cm³

Fill in the blanks. (4 marks)

㊺	5 200 cm² = _____ m²		㊻	1.85 m² = _____ cm²
㊼	4 560 000 cm³ = _____ m³		㊽	0.85 m³ = _____ cm³

Complete the table. (6 marks)

Line	Length to the nearest cm	Length to the nearest 0.5 cm
㊾ AB		
㊿ AC		
51 AD		

(Number line with points A, B, C, D marked)

Midway Test

Use the number cards below to solve the problems. (8 marks)

A	B	C	D	E	F	G	H	I
-6	4	5	-3	-12	6	-21	14	3

㊼ A − C = − 6 − 5 = _____

㊽ G ÷ D = _____ = _____

㊾ B + E = _____ = _____

㊿ E × F = _____ = _____

56 A × I = _____ = _____

57 E ÷ A = _____ = _____

58 G + I − E = _____ = _____

59 C − (A + H) = _____ = _____

Write an integer equation for each problem. Then solve the problems. (4 marks)

60 Two integers have a sum of +5. One of the integers is +12. What is the other integer?

The other integer is _____ .

61 The temperature dropped 11 °C from a high of 7 °C. What was the temperature after the drop?

The temperature was _____ °C.

Complete the table. (4 marks)

	Decimal	Fraction	Percent
62	1.6		
63			45%

Solve the problems. (4 marks)

64. Dave saved 38.5% of $70 and Steve saved 46.3% of $50. Who saved more money? How much more?

    _____ saved $_____ more than _____ .

65. Uncle Fred sold 85% of the 80 cakes he had.

    a. How many cakes did he sell? _____ cakes

    b. If he had sold 4 more cakes, what percent would he have sold altogether? _____%

Use the given formula to answer the questions. (2 marks)

66. **Steve's savings:**

    Savings = $78.50 − $6.50 × number of days

    a. How much will he have after 7 days? $_____

    b. How much will he have after 12 days? $_____

Coordinates

WORDS TO LEARN

Coordinate plane — a plane divided into 4 quadrants to represent ordered pairs of numbers as points

Linear equation — an equation represented by a straight line on a coordinate plane

Solution — the value of the variable(s) that makes the equation true

Write the ordered pair to show the location of each labelled point on the grid.

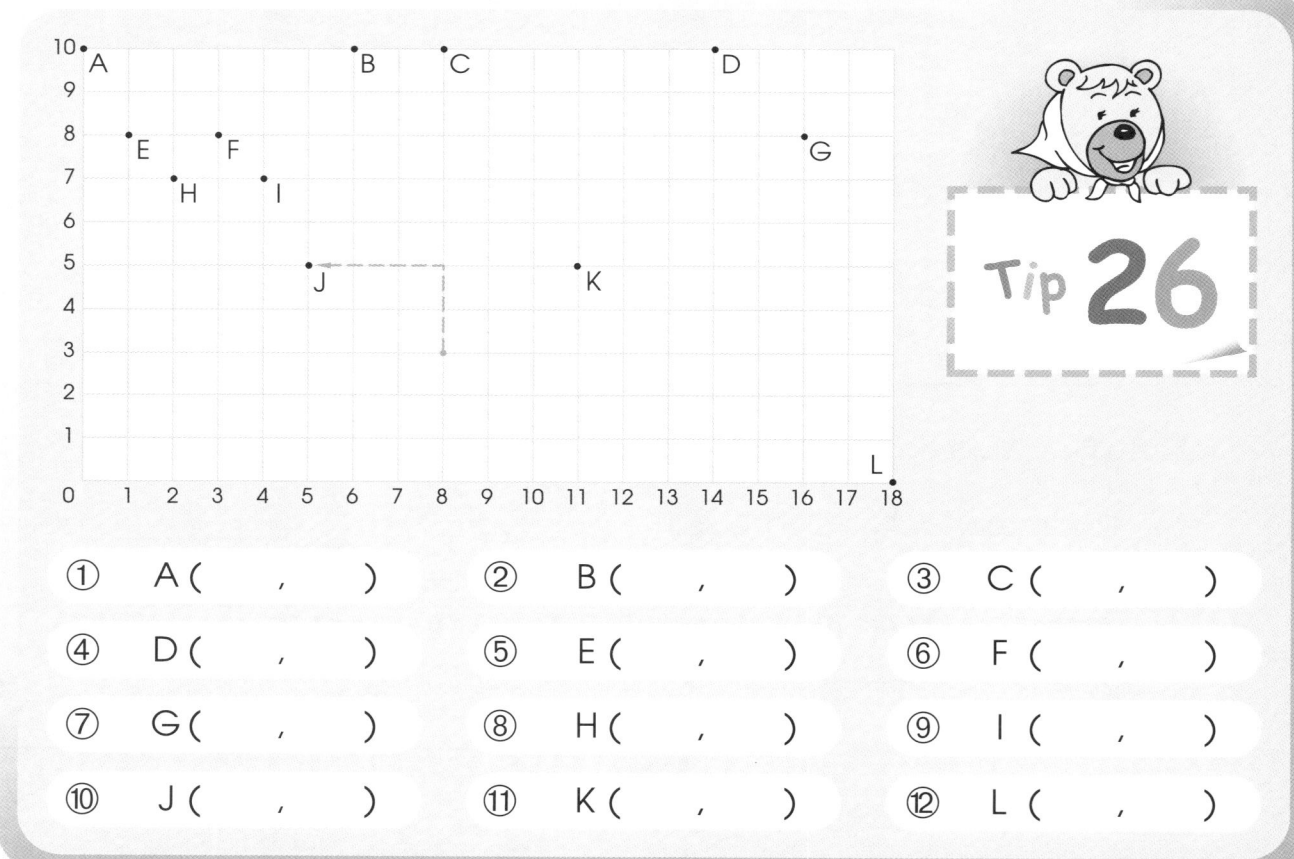

① A (,) ② B (,) ③ C (,)
④ D (,) ⑤ E (,) ⑥ F (,)
⑦ G (,) ⑧ H (,) ⑨ I (,)
⑩ J (,) ⑪ K (,) ⑫ L (,)

Follow Tony's method to locate each child on the grid above and find which letters they will reach.

I am at (8, 3). If I move 2 units up and 3 units left, I will reach point "J".

40 MATHSMART (GRADE 7)

⑬ Dave is at (3, 2). If he moves 5 units up and 1 unit right, he will reach point _____ .

⑭ Helen is at (0, 10). If she moves 8 units right, she will reach point _____ .

⑮ Elaine is at (9, 7). If she moves 7 units right and 1 unit up, she will reach point _____ .

⑯ Steve is at (16, 7). If he moves 5 units left and 2 units down, he will reach point _____ .

Use the coordinate plane below to answer the questions.

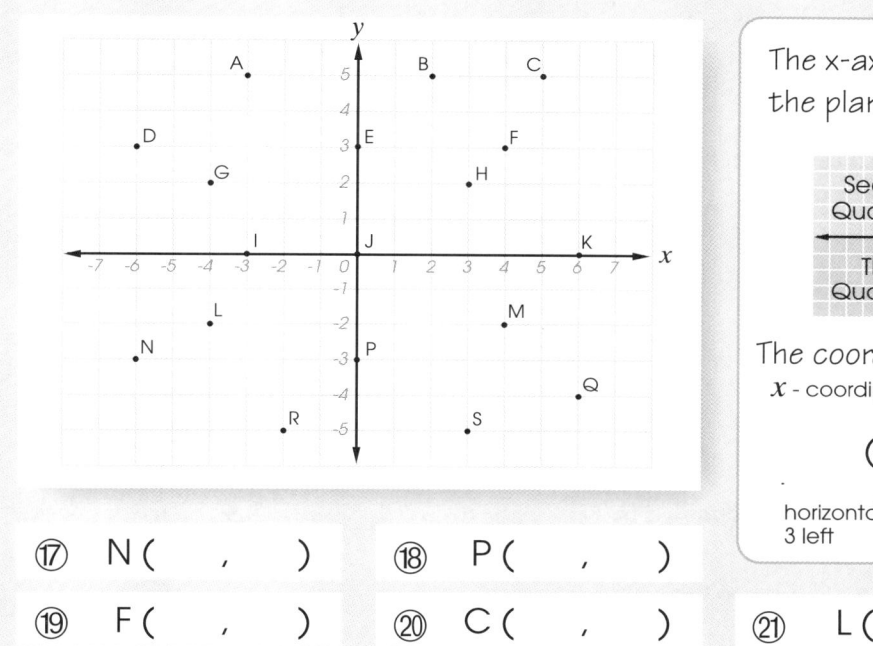
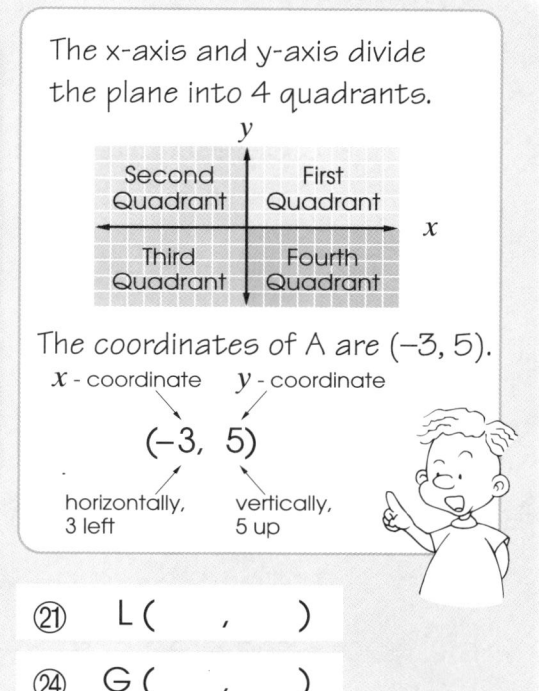

⑰ N (,)   ⑱ P (,)
⑲ F (,)   ⑳ C (,)   ㉑ L (,)
㉒ S (,)   ㉓ A (,)   ㉔ G (,)

㉕ Which points are in the first quadrant? _____

㉖ Which points are in the second quadrant? _____

㉗ Which points are in the third quadrant? _____

㉘ Which points are in the fourth quadrant? _____

㉙ Which points are on the x-axis? _____

㉚ Which points are on the y-axis? _____

Look at Tony's coordinate plane and answer the questions.

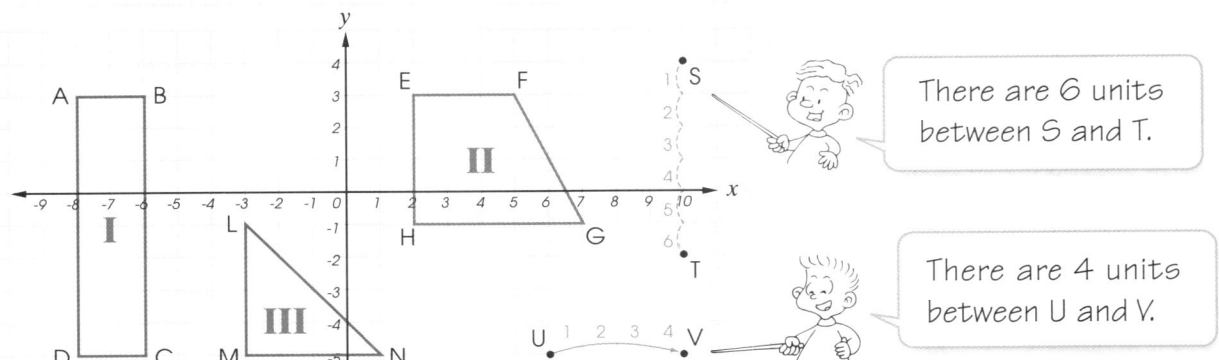

㉛ Write the ordered pairs of the vertices of shape I.

A (-8, 3), B (___ , ___), C (___ , ___), D (___ , ___)

㉜ Write the ordered pairs of the vertices of shape II.

E (___ , ___), F (___ , ___), G (___ , ___), H (___ , ___)

㉝ Write the ordered pairs of the vertices of shape III.

L (___ , ___), M (___ , ___), N (___ , ___)

㉞ a. How many units are between A and B? _____ units

b. How many units are between A and D? _____ units

c. What is the area of shape I? _____ square units

㉟ a. How many units are between E and F? _____ units

b. How many units are between G and H? _____ units

c. How many units are between E and H? _____ units

d. What is the area of shape II? _____ square units

㊱ a. How many units are between L and M? _____ units

b. How many units are between M and N? _____ units

c. What is the area of shape III? _____ square units

Follow Tony's method to complete the tables and draw the graphs. Then use the graphs to answer the questions.

$y = x + 2$

x	-1	0	2
y	1	2	4
	$y = -1 + 2$ $= 1$	$y = 0 + 2$ $= 2$	$y = 2 + 2$ $= 4$
(x, y)	(-1, 1)	(0, 2)	(2, 4)

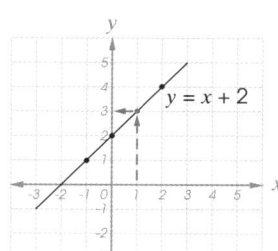

From the graph you can see that when $x = 1$, $y = 3$.

㊲ $y = x - 1$

a.
x	0	3	5
y			
(x, y)			

b. When $x = 4$, $y = $ _____ .

c. When $y = 1$, $x = $ _____ .

㊳ $y = 2x - 1$

a.
x	-1	1	3
y			
(x, y)			

b. When $x = 2$, $y = $ _____ .

c. When $y = -1$, $x = $ _____ .

ACTIVITY

Look at the graph and tick ✔ the right boxes.

1. Equation A is   ☐ $y = x + 1$ ☐ $y = x + 2$

2. Equation B is   ☐ $x = 1$ ☐ $y = 1$

3. The point of intersection of equations A and B is
   ☐ (1, 3)   ☐ (3, 1)

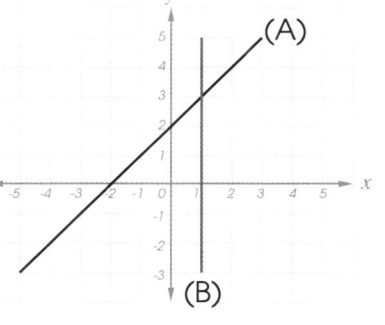

More about Algebraic Expressions

WORDS TO LEARN

Term — a mathematical expression that is either a number or the product of a number and one or more variables

Variable — an unknown value represented by a letter

Literal part — the variable part of a term

e.g. $3x^2 + 5$

Term: $3x^2$, $+5$ Literal part of $3x^2$: x^2

Evaluate — find out an idea of the amount or value of something

Formula — a general rule showing how variables are related to one another

Read what the children say. Then write in algebraic expressions.

①  A number 25 less than the square of y. _____

②  The sum of 25 and y, divided by 5. _____

③  The sum of 25 and the square of y. _____

④  The square of the difference between y and 25. _____

⑤  The sum of 25 and y, multiplied by 2. _____

⑥  Subtract 25 from the product of y and 25. _____

Evaluate for _y_ = 6.

⑦ 2y + 12 = _____ ⑧ y^2 + y = _____

⑨ 9(y – 2) = _____ ⑩ (10.5 – y) ÷ 5 = _____

Evaluate for _m_ = 2 and _n_ = -2.

⑪ 2m – 4n = _____ ⑫ mn – 7 = _____

⑬ (m + n)(m – n) = _____ ⑭ $m^2 + n^2$ = _____

Read what Tony says. Then help him complete the table.

Expression : $2y^2 - 3y + 7$
Terms : $2y^2$, –3y, 7
No. of terms : 3

An algebraic expression can be considered as the sum of the terms.
i.e. $2y^2$ + (–3y) + 7

	Expression	Terms	No. of Terms
⑮	$5x^2 + 3x + 2y - 8$		
⑯	3a + 2b – 6		
⑰	0.5m + 2n – 2p + 9		
⑱	$8u^3 - 4u^2 + 3$		

Write whether the terms are like or unlike.

⑲ x^2, $3x^2$ and $-0.5x^2$ are _____ terms.

⑳ –3y, y^2 and 2y are _____ terms.

㉑ 4m, $\frac{3}{4}$m, 0.6m and –m are _____ terms.

㉒ 10xy, $-2xy^2$, $\frac{9}{5}$xy and xy^2 are _____ terms.

Follow Helen's method to simplify the expressions.

> We can use the distributive law to combine like terms.
> 5x and 2x are like terms; 9 and -4 are like terms.

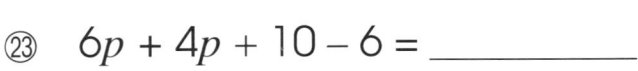

$5x + 9 + 2x - 4$
$= 5x + 2x + 9 - 4$
$= (5 + 2)x + 5$
$= 7x + 5$

㉓ $6p + 4p + 10 - 6 =$ _____

㉔ $8d - 2d - 2 + 15 =$ _____

㉕ $3k - 12k - 3 - 6 =$ _____

㉖ $\frac{3}{4}m + \frac{1}{2}m + 4 - 11 =$ _____

㉗ $8n^2 - 6n + 7n^2 - 4n + 5 =$ _____

㉘ $3a + 4b - 9a + 4 - b =$ _____

㉙ $m + 2n - 6n + 8m + 5 =$ _____

㉚ $2pq + 4p + 3p - 6pq - 7p =$ _____

㉛ $6x^2y + 5y - x^2y + 3y - 6y =$ _____

Tip 32

Simplify the expressions.

㉜ $3(x + 5) - 6$

= ___ x + ___

㉝ $5y - 2(y + 1)$

= _____

㉞ $6(h - 2) + 2h$

= _____

㉟ $-2(m + 7) + 10$

= _____

㊱ $8n + 4(3 - n)$

= _____

㊲ $3(p + 4) + 2(p - 2)$

= _____

Evaluate for $n = 3$.

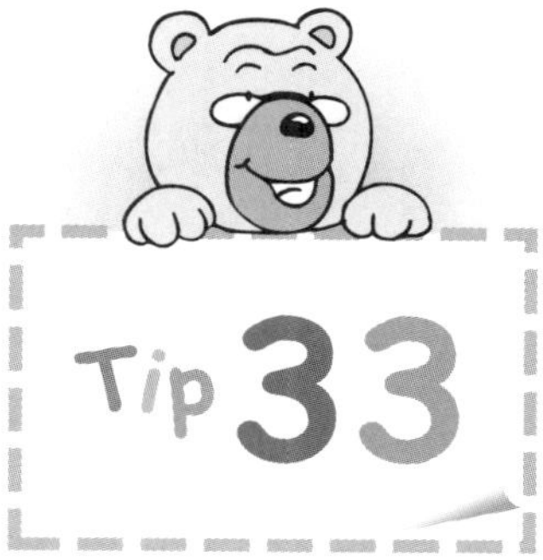

㊳ $3n + 2n$ = ______ ㊴ $4n + 1 - 2n$ = ______

㊵ $n^2 + 3n^2$ = ______ ㊶ $10 - 5n + 5$ = ______

Evaluate for $a = -2$.

㊷ $6a - 2a$ = ______ ㊸ $9 - 3a + 2a$ = ______

㊹ $5a^2 - 3a^2$ = ______ ㊺ $2(a - 2) + 7$ = ______

Evaluate for $d = 0.2$.

㊻ $10 - 2(d - 3)$ = ______ ㊼ $7d + 2(d - 2)$ = ______

㊽ $3(d - 1) + 9$ = ______ ㊾ $6d^2 + 3d^2 - 4d^2$ = ______

Read what the children say. Then substitute the values for the letters and calculate.

㊿ Evaluate:

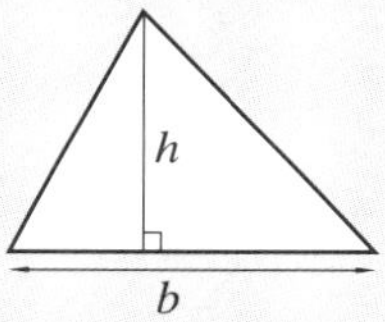

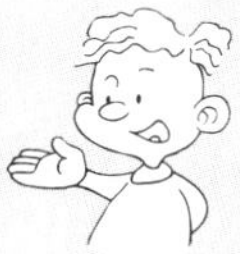

The area of a triangle is found with this formula:

$A = \frac{1}{2}bh$

a. $h = 4,\ b = 9$ $A =$ ______ b. $h = 10,\ b = 12$ $A =$ ______

c. $h = 8,\ b = 4$ $A =$ ______ d. $h = 32,\ b = 24$ $A =$ ______

(51) Evaluate:

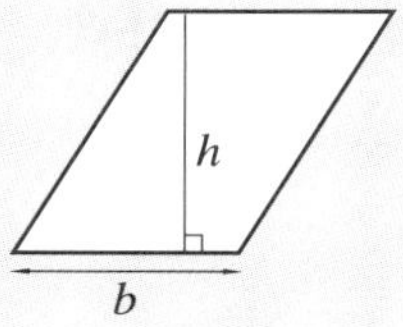

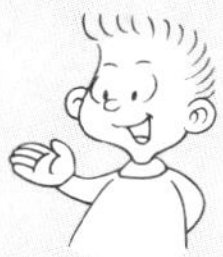

The area of a parallelogram is found with this formula:

$A = bh$

a. $h = 5,\ b = 9$ $A =$ ______ b. $h = 9,\ b = 4$ $A =$ ______

c. $h = 12,\ b = 30$ $A =$ ______ d. $h = 1,\ b = 10$ $A =$ ______

㊾ **Evaluate:**

The volume of a rectangular block is found with this formula:

$V = lwh$

a. $l = 3$, $w = 5$, $h = 4$ $V = $ _____
b. $l = 5$, $w = 10$, $h = 2$ $V = $ _____
c. $l = 0.5$, $w = 4$, $h = 7$ $V = $ _____
d. $l = 0.2$, $w = 3$, $h = 0.5$ $V = $ _____

㊼ **Evaluate:**

$P = \dfrac{r}{n} \times 100\%$

Use this formula to find the percent scored on a test, where r = number of right answers and n = number of problems.

a. $r = 70$, $n = 80$ $P = $ _____
b. $r = 65$, $n = 200$ $P = $ _____
c. $r = 30$, $n = 32$ $P = $ _____
d. $r = 36$, $n = 45$ $P = $ _____

Solve the equations and check the answers.

㊾ $3y + 5y = 16$

Check: $3(\_\_\_) + 5(\_\_\_) = 16$

㊺ $x - 7 + 4 = 6$

Check: $(\_\_\_) - 7 + 4 = 6$

㊻ $8m - 6m = -12$

Check: $8(\_\_\_) - 6(\_\_\_) = -12$

㊽ $8a - 12a + 6a = 14$

Check: $8(\_\_\_) - 12(\_\_\_) + 6(\_\_\_) = 14$

48   MATHSMART (GRADE 7)

Help Uncle Fred complete the equations for his problems. Then find the answers.

58. 3 beams and a $14 saw came to $38. How much did each beam cost?

    _____ y + _____ = _____

    Each beam cost $_____ .

59. 4 bags of sand and 20 kg of cement weigh 100 kg altogether, how heavy is one bag of sand?

    _____ m + _____ = _____

    One bag of sand is _____ kg.

60. I work 8 hours a day and 5 days a week. If I earn $500 a week, how much do I earn an hour?

    _____ x _____ p = _____

    Uncle Fred earns $_____ an hour.

ACTIVITY

Circle the three correct number cards to solve Tony's riddle.

The sum of three numbers is 27. The second number is double the first. The third number is one less than the first. What are the numbers?

10	7	4
16	5	14
6	12	8

11 Angles and Lines

WORDS TO LEARN

Adjacent angles — the two angles that share a common side and vertex and do not overlap

Complementary angles — two adjacent angles that have a sum of 90°

Supplementary angles — two adjacent angles that have a sum of 180°

Opposite angles — the opposite and congruent angles formed by two intersecting lines

Transversal — a line intersecting two or more lines

Parallel lines — two or more lines that are in the same plane and do not intersect (symbol: ⫽)

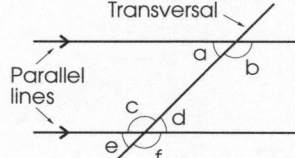

Alternate angles: ∠a = ∠d, ∠b = ∠c

Corresponding angles: ∠a = ∠e, ∠b = ∠f

Measure the angles and tell whether they are adjacent, complementary, supplementary or opposite.

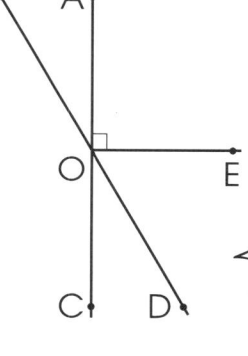

① ∠BOA = _____ , ∠AOE = _____

They are _____ angles.

② ∠BOA = _____ , ∠DOC = _____

They are _____ angles.

③ ∠COD = _____ , ∠DOE = _____

They are _____ angles.

④ ∠BOA = _____ , ∠AOD = _____

They are _____ angles.

Tip 34

Tip 35

50 MATHSMART (GRADE 7)

Find the value of the unknown angles.

⑤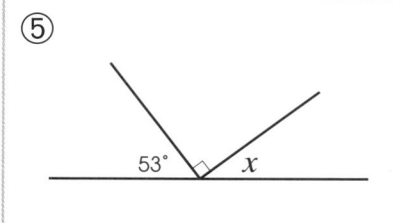

x = _____

⑥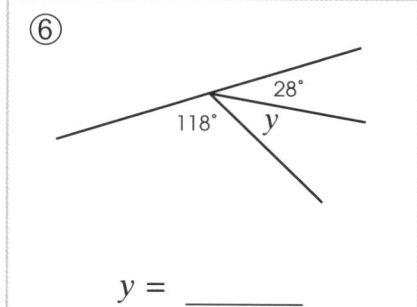

y = _____

⑦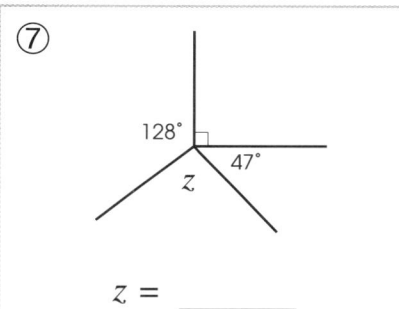

z = _____

⑧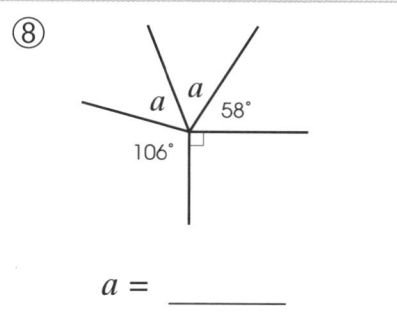

a = _____

⑨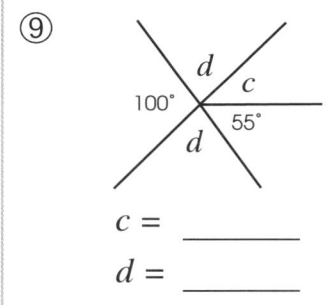

c = _____
d = _____

⑩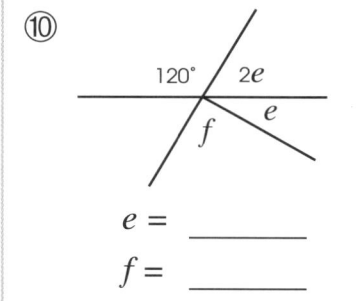

e = _____
f = _____

⑪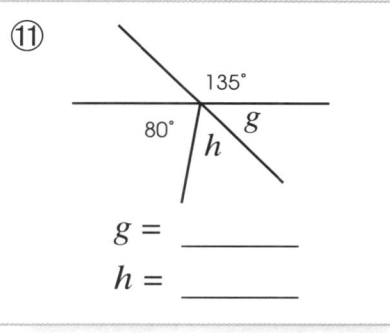

g = _____
h = _____

⑫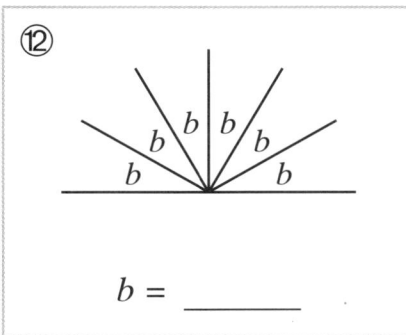

b = _____

⑬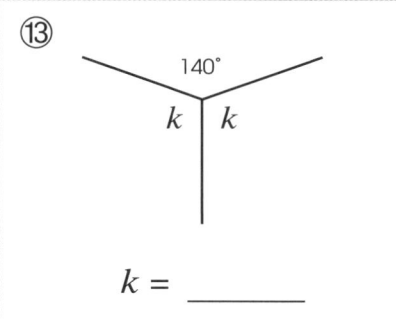

k = _____

⑭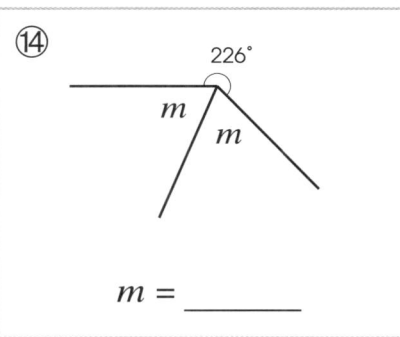

m = _____

⑮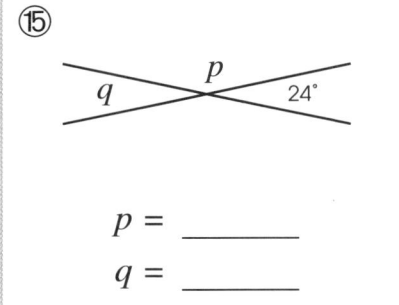

p = _____
q = _____

⑯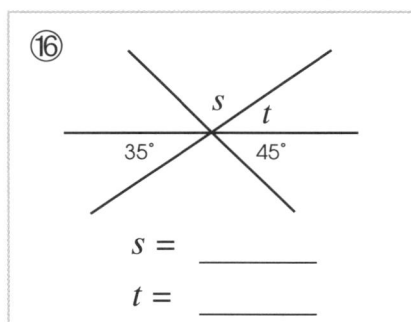

s = _____
t = _____

⑰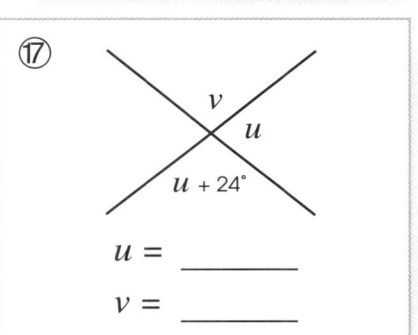

u = _____
v = _____

Follow Tony's method to tell whether the angles are corresponding or alternate.

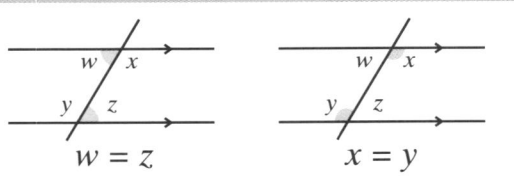

a and *c* are corresponding angles;
b and *d* are corresponding angles too.

w and *z* are alternate angles;
x and *y* are alternate angles too.

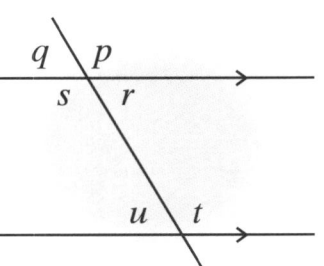

⑱ *p* and *t* are _____ angles.

⑲ *s* and *t* are _____ angles.

⑳ *u* and *r* are _____ angles.

㉑ *q* and *u* are _____ angles.

Find the value of the angles.

㉒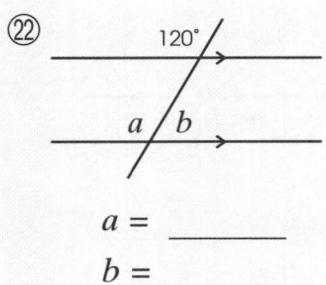

a = ____
b = ____

㉓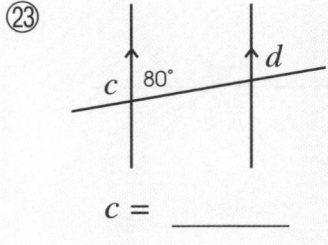

c = ____
d = ____

㉔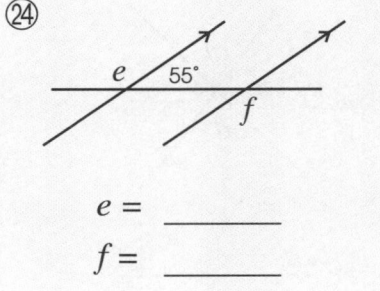

e = ____
f = ____

㉕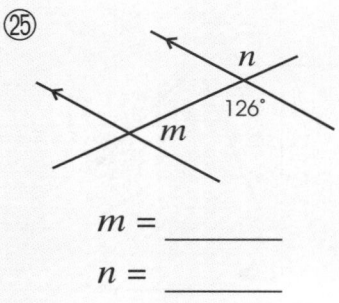

m = ____
n = ____

㉖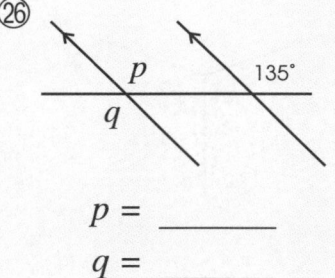

p = ____
q = ____

㉗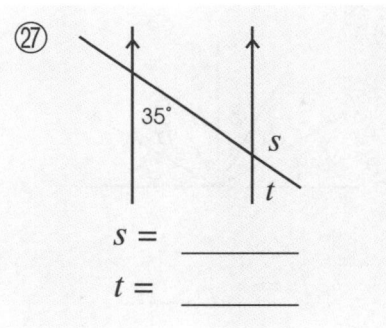

s = ____
t = ____

㉘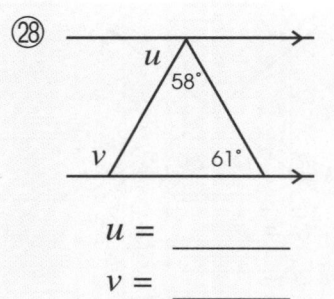

u = ____
v = ____

㉙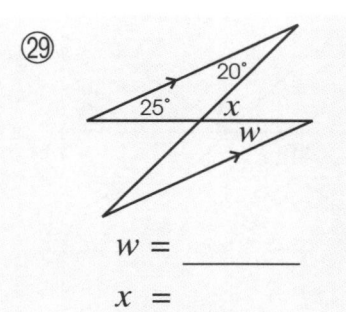

w = ____
x = ____

㉚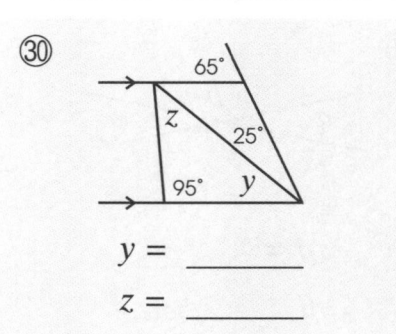

y = ____
z = ____

Follow the children's methods to find the marked angles.

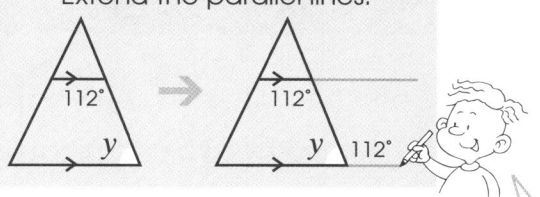

Extend the parallel lines.

It is easier to find the answer by extending the parallel lines.
$y = 180° − 112° = 68°$

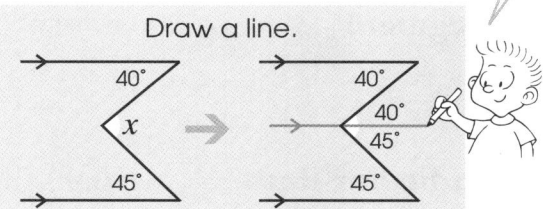

You can add a parallel line.
$x = 40° + 45° = 85°$

Draw a line.

③①
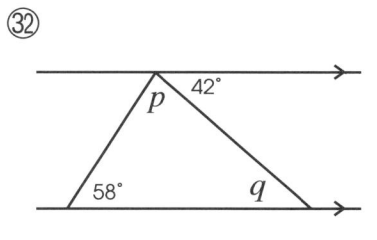

$x = $ _____
$y = $ _____

③②

$p = $ _____
$q = $ _____

③③
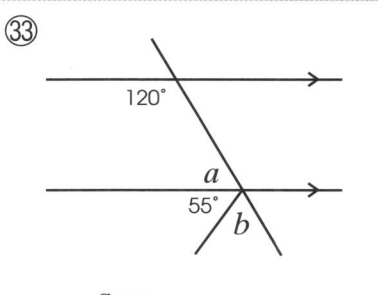

$a = $ _____
$b = $ _____

③④
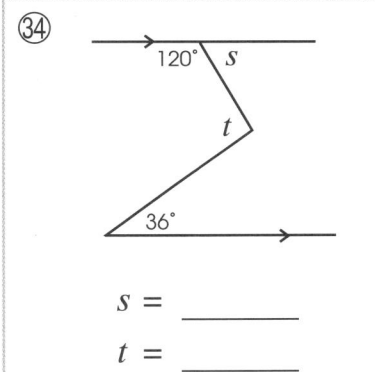

$s = $ _____
$t = $ _____

③⑤
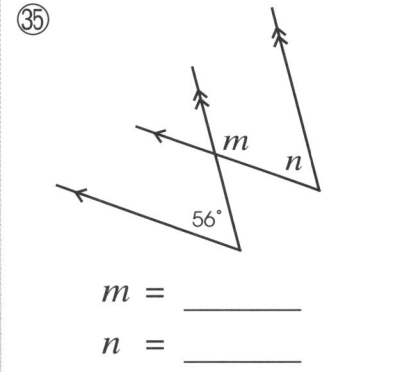

$m = $ _____
$n = $ _____

③⑥
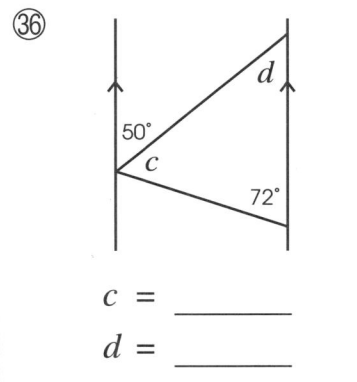

$c = $ _____
$d = $ _____

ACTIVITY

Look at the lines and tick ✔ the right answers.

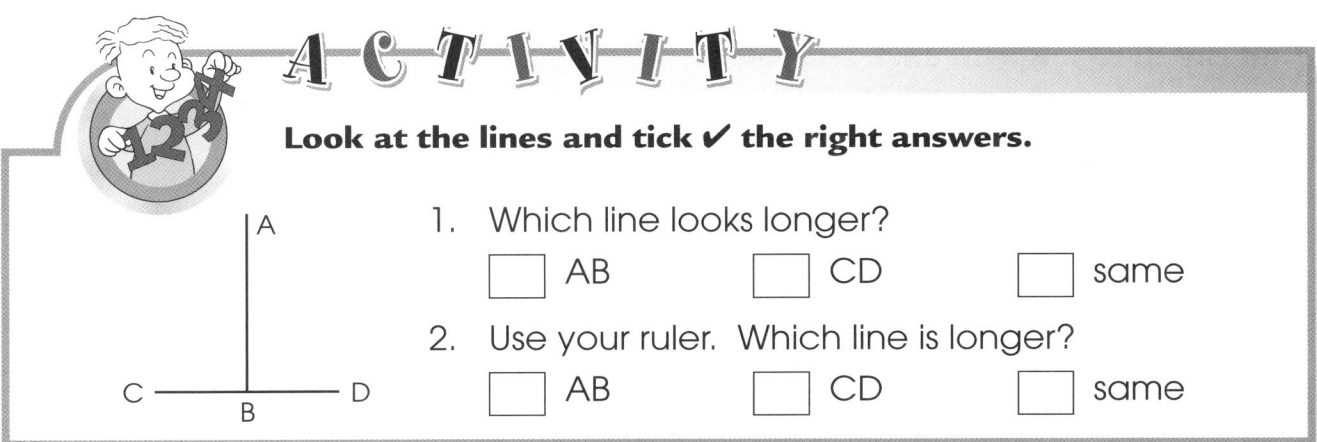

1. Which line looks longer?
   ☐ AB   ☐ CD   ☐ same
2. Use your ruler. Which line is longer?
   ☐ AB   ☐ CD   ☐ same

12 Angles and Shapes

WORDS TO LEARN

Bisector — a line that divides an angle or a line into two equal parts

Line segment — a part of a line bounded and named by two end points

e.g. A●────────●B   segment AB or $\overline{AB}$

Perpendicular lines — two lines that intersect to form right angles

Use a protractor to measure the angles in each triangle and find their sum. Then tell whether the triangle is scalene, isosceles or equilateral.

①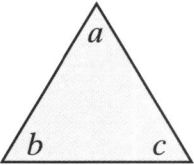

∠a = _____ ∠b = _____ ∠c = _____

∠a + ∠b + ∠c = _____

_____ triangle

②

∠l = _____ ∠m = _____ ∠n = _____

∠l + ∠m + ∠n = _____

_____ triangle

③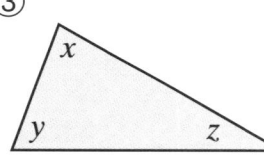

∠x = _____ ∠y = _____ ∠z = _____

∠x + ∠y + ∠z = _____

_____ triangle

Tip 38

Tip 39

Find the third angle of each triangle.

④ 60°, 25°, _____   ⑤ 36°, 115°, _____   ⑥ 82°, 82°, _____

⑦ 64°, 32°, _____   ⑧ 120°, 20°, _____   ⑨ 45°, 110°, _____

⑩ 70°, 62°, _____   ⑪ 23°, 86°, _____   ⑫ 33°, 52°, _____

⑬ 45°, 45°, _____   ⑭ 90°, 38°, _____   ⑮ 120°, 15°, _____

Follow Tony's method to construct the triangles.

Construct a triangle with sides 4 cm, 5 cm and 6 cm.
- **1st** Draw a line segment AB = 6 cm.
- **2nd** Take A as the centre and a compass radius of 5 cm; draw an arc.
- **3rd** Take B as the centre and a compass radius of 4 cm; draw an arc to cut the first arc at point C.
- **4th** Join AC and BC, and you can get △ABC.

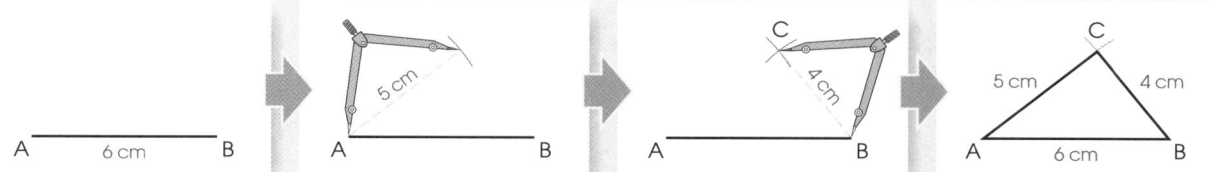

⑯ Construct an equilateral triangle with sides 3cm.

⑰ Construct a triangle with sides 3cm, 4cm and 5cm.

⑱ Construct an isosceles triangle with 2 sides 4cm and 1 side 2cm.

⑲ Construct a triangle with sides 2cm, 5cm and 6cm.

⑳ Construct an isosceles triangle with 2 sides 5.5cm each and 1 side 10cm.

Follow Dave's method to construct a perpendicular bisector for each line segment.

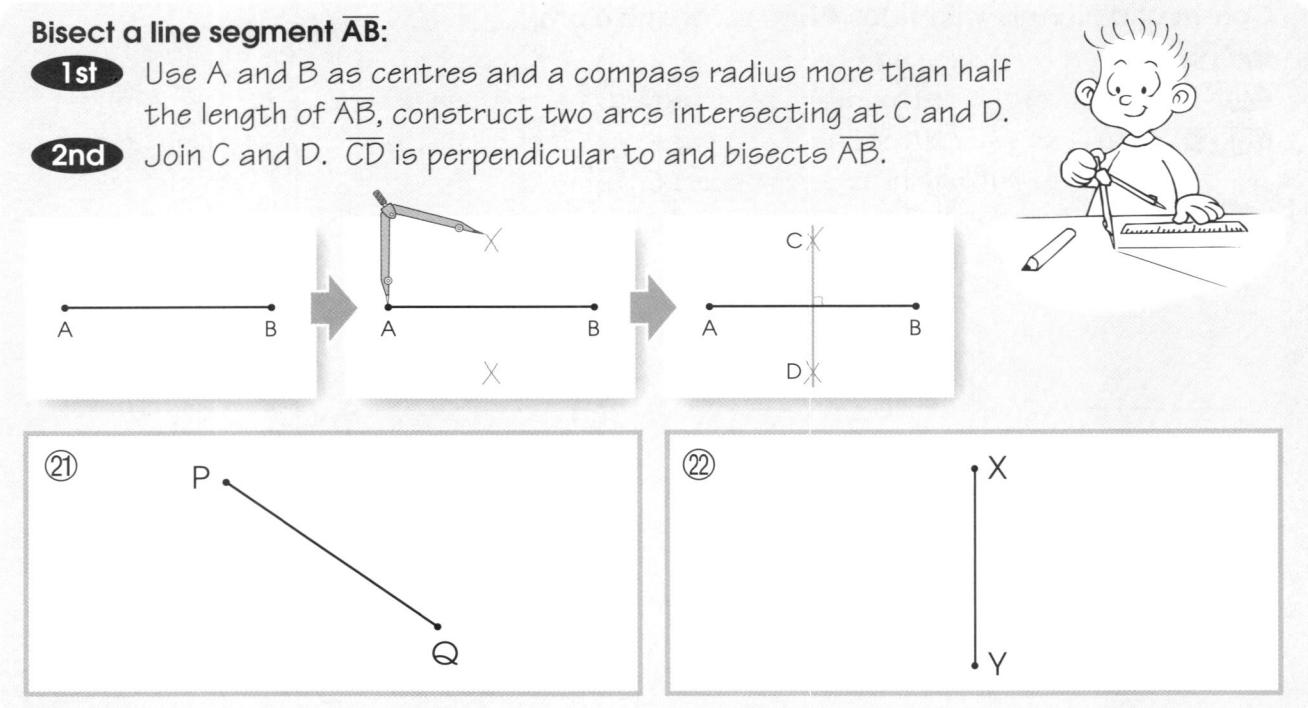

Follow Helen's method to construct an angle bisector for each angle.

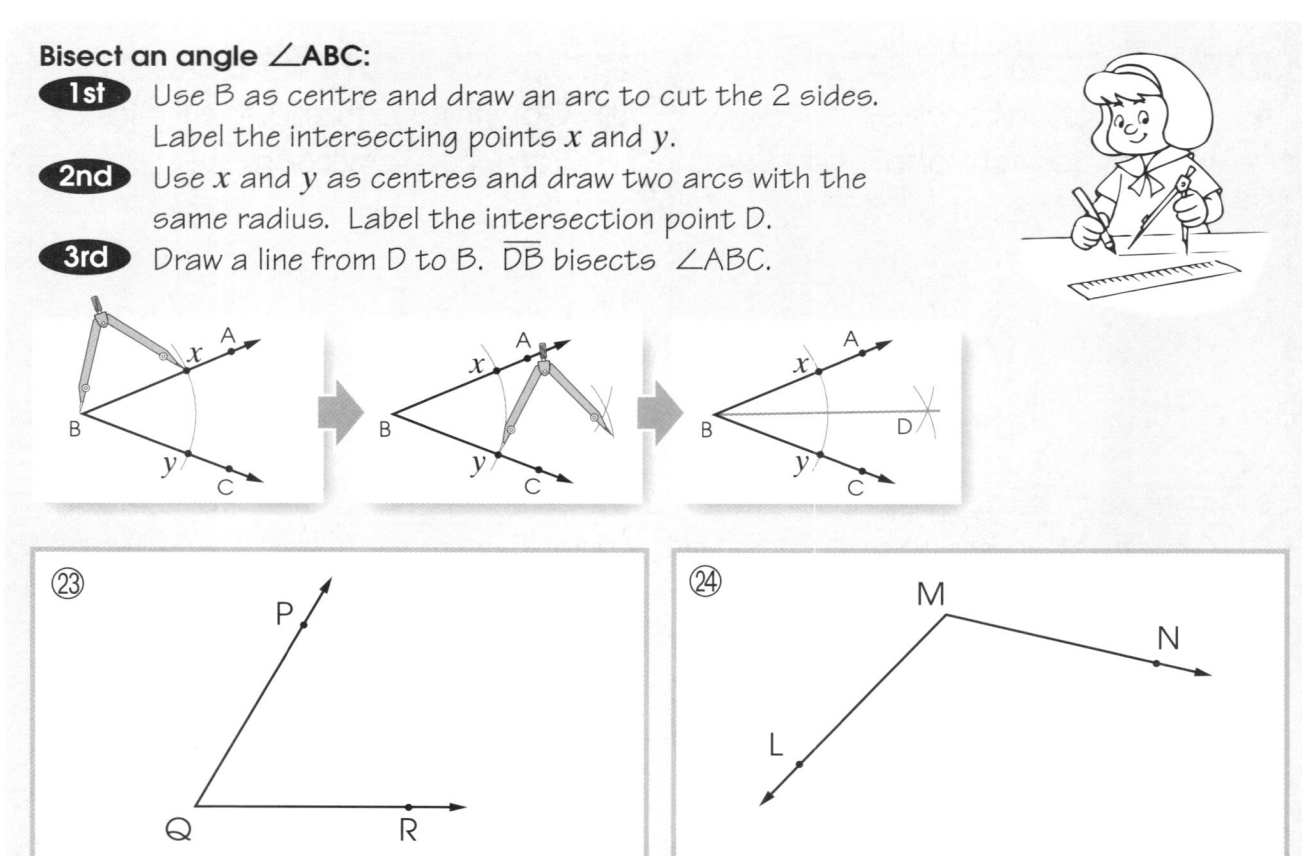

Read what Tony says. Then tell whether each pair of triangles is congruent or similar.

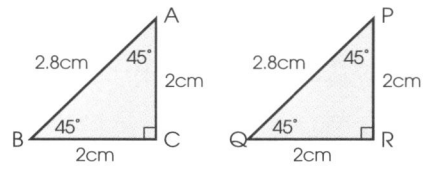 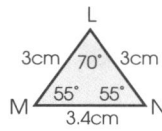 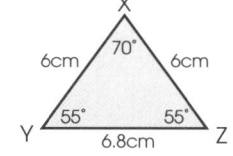

△ABC and △PQR have the same size and shape. They are congruent.

△LMN and △XYZ have the same shape but different sizes. They are similar.

△ABC and △PQR are congruent triangles. △LMN and △XYZ are similar triangles.

㉕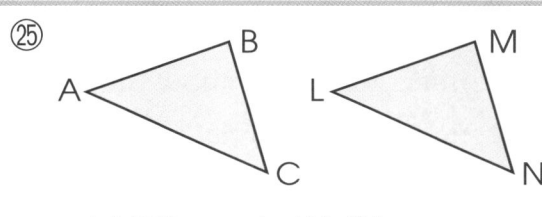

△ABC and △LMN are _____ triangles.

㉖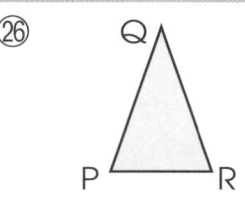

△PQR and △STU are _____ triangles.

㉗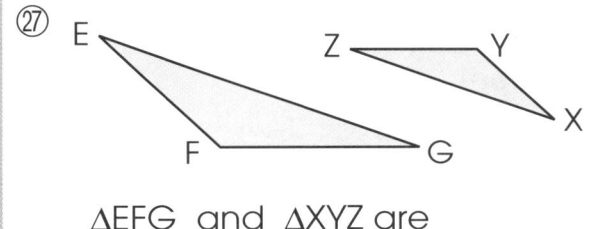

△EFG and △XYZ are _____ triangles.

㉘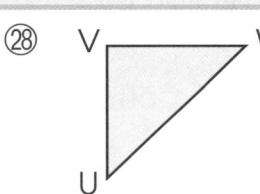

△UVW and △JKL are _____ triangles.

ACTIVITY

Find the lengths of the triangles.

1. △ABC and △DEF are similar triangles.

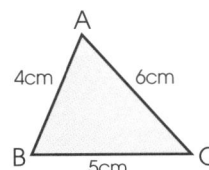 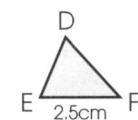

DE = _____ cm

DF = _____ cm

2. △PQR and △XYZ are similar triangles.

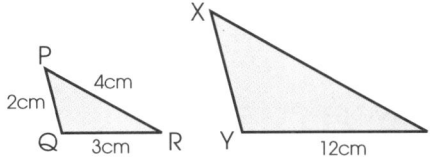

XY = _____ cm

XZ = _____ cm

Tip 40

MathSmart (Grade 7)

Statistics

WORDS TO LEARN

Frequency	-	the number of times an event occurs within a period
Frequency distribution	-	a table showing the frequency of different groups of data
Circle graph	-	a graph using parts of a circle to show information about a whole
Histogram	-	a bar graph using connected bars to show the frequency of occurrence of grouped data
Broken-line graph	-	a graph made by joining successive plotted points

Look at the broken-line graph and answer the questions.

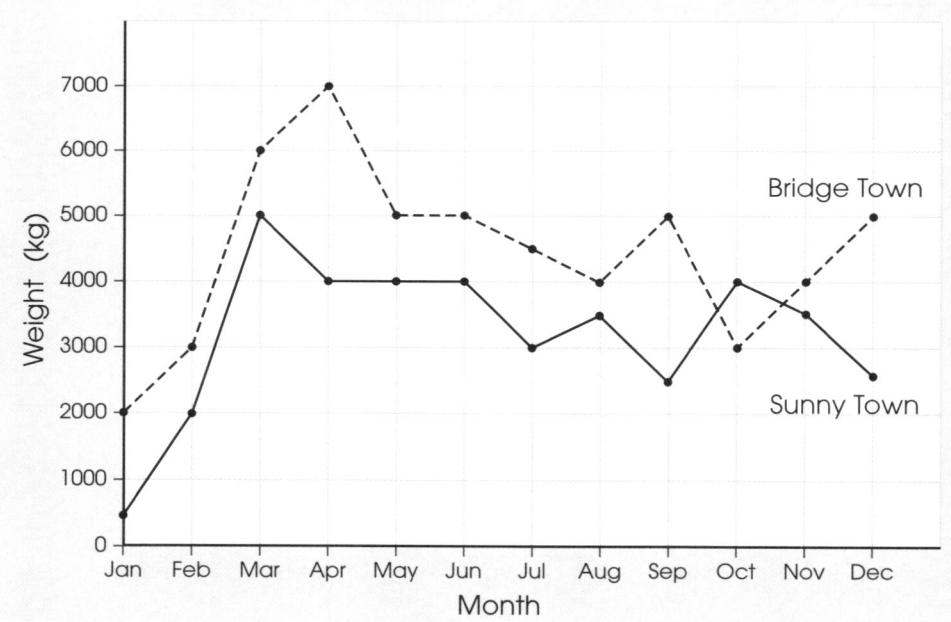

① How many more kilograms of waste paper were collected from Bridge Town than from Sunny Town in September? _____ kg

② How many more kilograms of waste paper were collected from Bridge Town in March than in August? _____ kg

58 MathSmart (Grade 7)

③ In which month was the greatest increase in the weight of waste paper collected from Sunny Town? _____

④ In which month was there the greatest difference in weight between the waste paper collected from Bridge Town and that from Sunny Town? _____

Use the circle graph and your protractor to find the percent of waste paper collected from different towns.

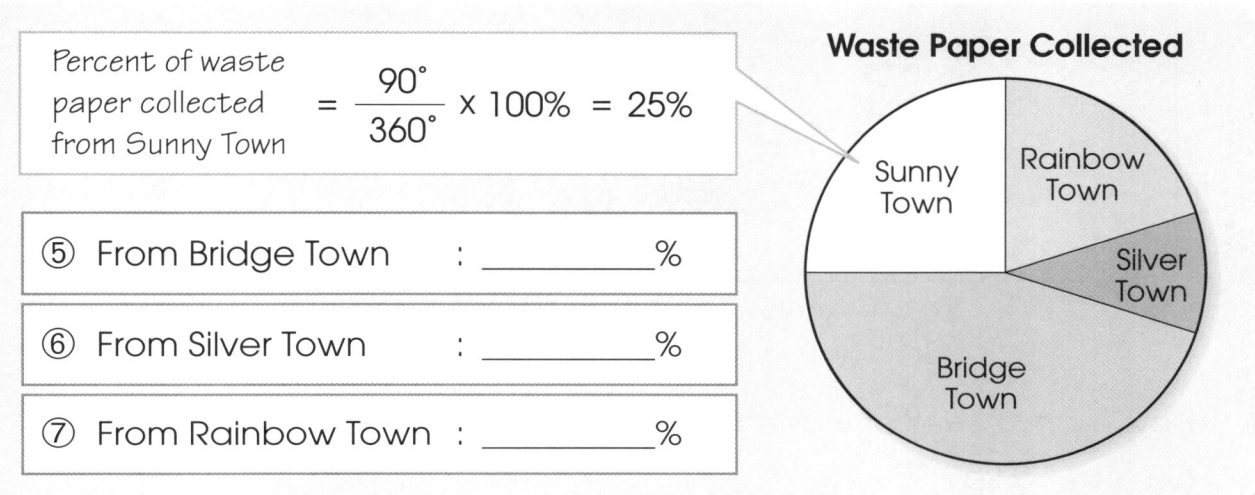

Percent of waste paper collected from Sunny Town = $\frac{90°}{360°}$ × 100% = 25%

⑤ From Bridge Town : _____ %

⑥ From Silver Town : _____ %

⑦ From Rainbow Town : _____ %

Follow Dave's method to find the size of angle for each item and complete the circle graph.

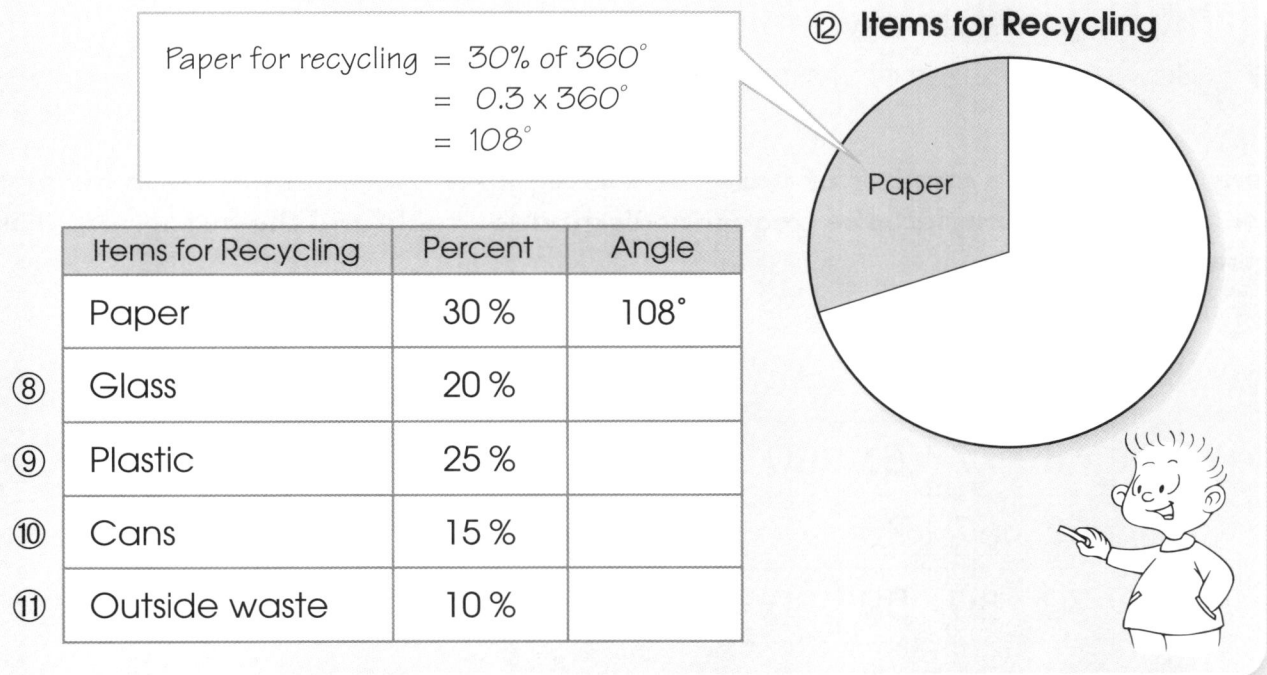

Paper for recycling = 30% of 360°
= 0.3 × 360°
= 108°

⑫ Items for Recycling

Items for Recycling	Percent	Angle
Paper	30 %	108°
⑧ Glass	20 %	
⑨ Plastic	25 %	
⑩ Cans	15 %	
⑪ Outside waste	10 %	

Use the histogram to answer the questions.

Number of Boxes of Waste Paper Collected

⑬ How many boxes of waste paper weighed between 6.0 and 7.9 kg? _____

⑭ How many boxes of waste paper weighed under 3.9 kg? _____

⑮ How many boxes of waste paper weighed over 8.0 kg? _____

⑯ How many boxes of waste paper were collected? _____

Tony recorded the number of boxes of waste paper collected weekly in his area. Use the data to complete the frequency distribution table and the histogram. Then answer the questions.

Number of boxes of waste paper collected weekly									
68	77	61	80	71	70	78	56	78	75
62	67	73	77	80	79	69	78	75	66
70	80	59	80	72	65	77	68	79	79

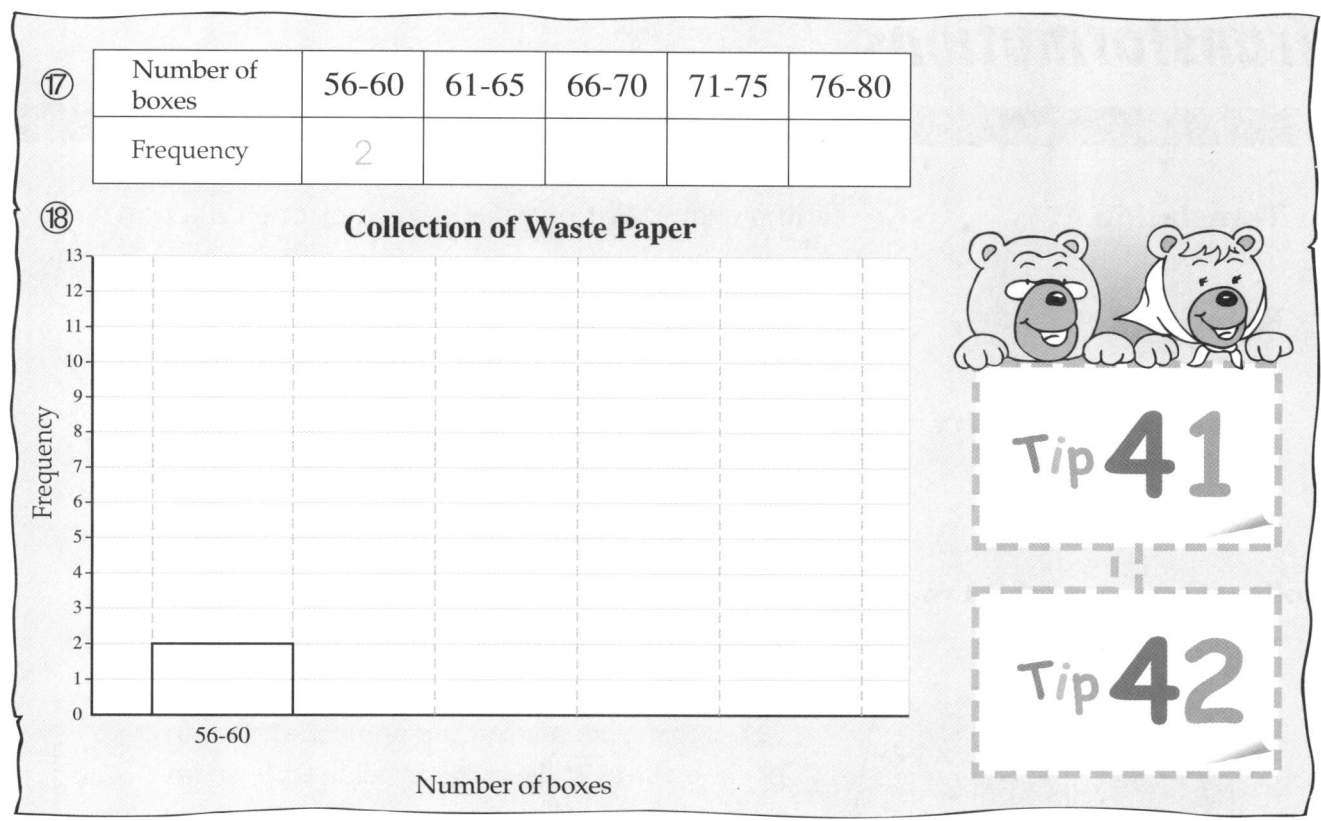

⑰
Number of boxes	56-60	61-65	66-70	71-75	76-80
Frequency	2				

⑱ **Collection of Waste Paper**

⑲ What is shown on the vertical axis? _____

⑳ What is shown on the horizontal axis? _____

㉑ How long did Tony take to collect the data? _____ weeks

ACTIVITY

Tick ✓ the chart that shows different information from the other two.

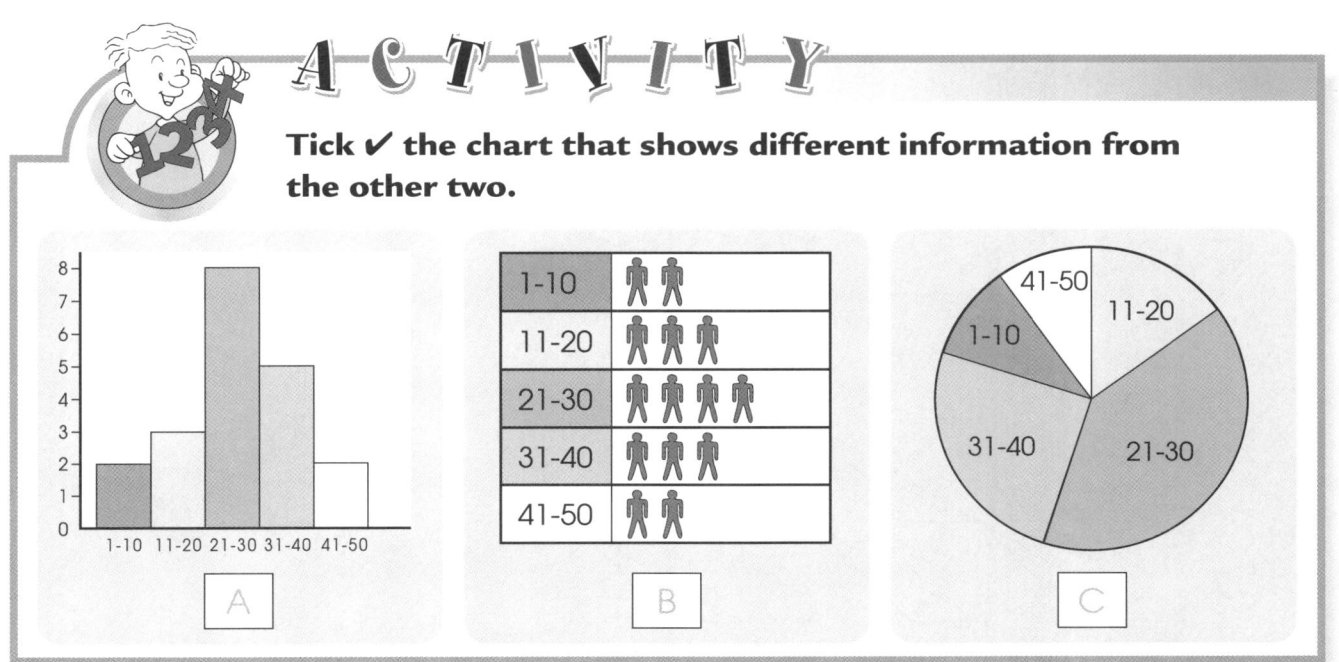

14 Transformations

WORDS TO LEARN

Translation	- sliding each point of a plane in the same direction and distance
Rotation	- turning the points of a plane about a fixed point
Reflection	- flipping the points of a plane over a line
Rotational symmetry	- a figure has rotational symmetry if its image fits onto itself in less than one full turn

Follow Dave's method to draw each reflection image in line *l*.

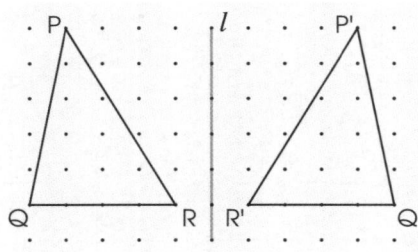

For point P, locate another point P' on the other side and at the same distance from l, so that $\overline{PP'}$ is perpendicular to l. Locate Q' and R' in the same way.

①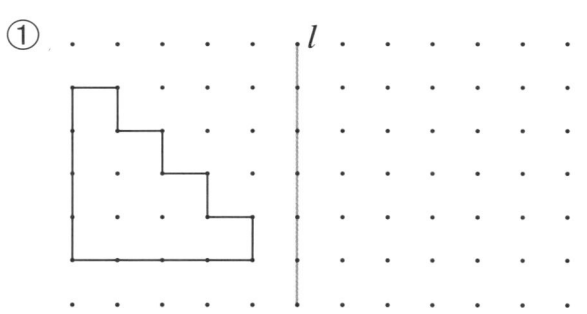

②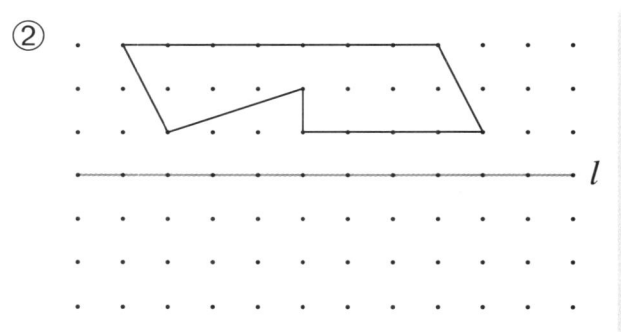

Follow Elaine's method to describe the translation images of the shaded triangle.

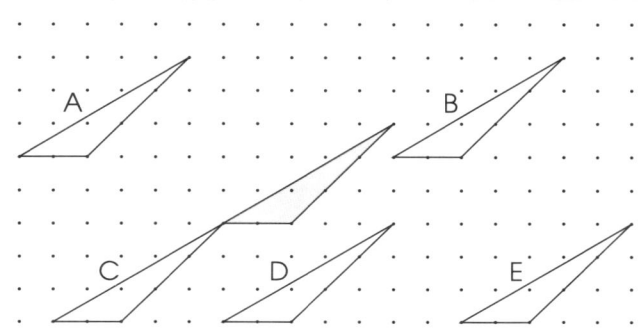

Image A: 6 units to the left and 2 units up.

③ Image B : _____

④ Image C : _____

⑤ Image D : _____

⑥ Image E : _____

Each triangle below is a rotation image of the shaded figure. Find the coordinates of the turning point, angle and direction of rotation.

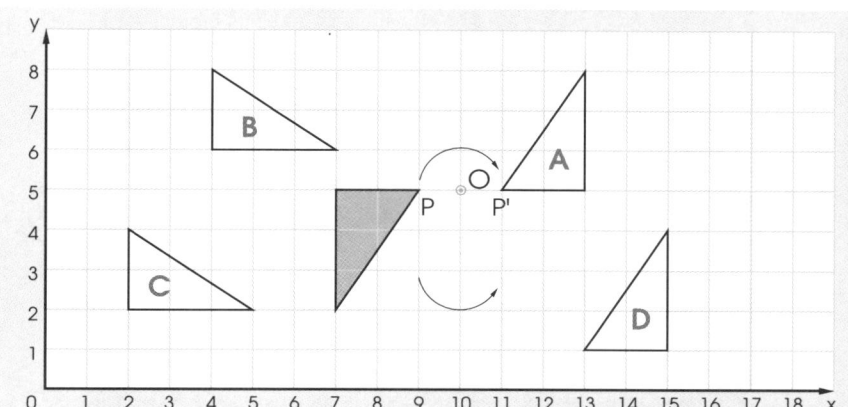

For rotation image A: The coordinates of the turning point O are (10, 5). The angle of rotation is 180° and the direction of rotation is counter clockwise or clockwise.

	Image	Turning Point	Angle and Direction of Rotation
⑦	B		
⑧	C		
⑨	D		

ACTIVITY

For each figure with rotational symmetry, find the order of symmetry.

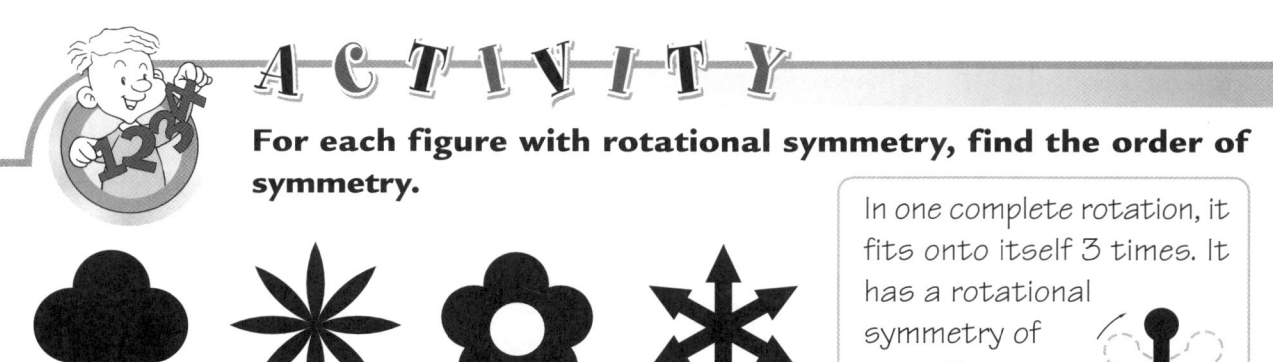

In one complete rotation, it fits onto itself 3 times. It has a rotational symmetry of order 3.

Shape	A	B	C	D
Order of Symmetry				

15 Probability

WORDS TO LEARN

Mutually exclusive events - events which do not have common outcomes
Independent events - events with no effect on one another

Read what Uncle Fred says. Then help Tony find the probabilities.

Tony wants a 🪶. The probability of getting a 🪶 is $\frac{1}{8}$. P(🪶) = $\frac{1}{8}$ = $\frac{\text{No. of favourable outcomes}}{\text{No. of possible outcomes}}$

① P(🐱) =

② P(🚗) =

③ P(🪶 or 🐱) =

④ P(Next Time! or Thank You!) =

⑤ P(🚗 or 🐶) =

There are 8 cards. One card is drawn at random each time. Find the probabilities.

⑥ P(1) =   ⑦ P(2) =

⑧ P(3) =   ⑨ P(7) =

⑩ P(1 or 7) =   ⑪ P(2 or 3) =

⑫ P(4 or 2) =   ⑬ P(not 7) =

Cards: 1 2 3 4 / 3 2 2 7

Tip 43

Follow Elaine's method to make a tree diagram and find the number of possible outcomes. Then find the probabilities.

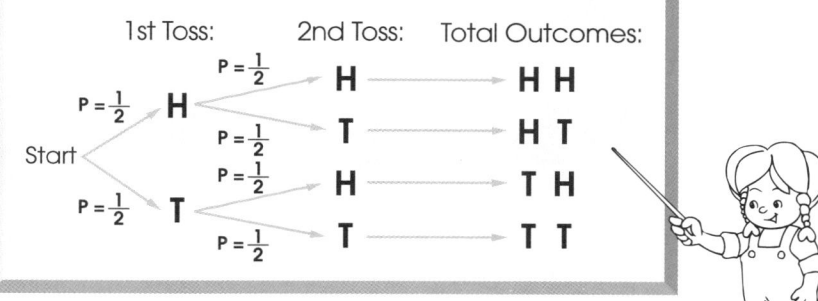

When I toss a coin twice, there are 4 possible outcomes.
$P(H \text{ and } H) = P(H) \times P(H)$
$= \dfrac{1}{2} \times \dfrac{1}{2}$
$= \dfrac{1}{4}$

⑭ The spinner is spun twice.

a. Number of possible outcomes = ☐

b. P (the two numbers are the same) = ☐

c. P (the two numbers are even) = ☐

⑮ A coin is tossed and a dice is thrown once.

a. Number of possible outcomes = ☐

b. P (head and 3) = ☐   c. P (tail and 6) = ☐

d. P (head and >4) = ☐   e. P (tail and 3 or 4) = ☐

Tip 44

ACTIVITY

Find the probabilities and tick ✔ the right ☐.

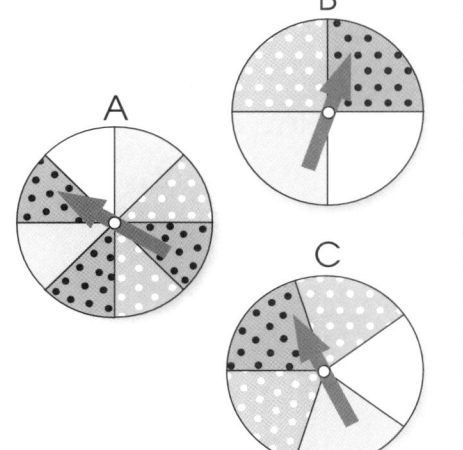

1. Find the probability of spinning ▓ on each spinning wheel.

   A ☐   B ☐   C ☐

2. If you want to win a game by spinning ▓, which wheel would you like to spin?

   A ☐   B ☐   C ☐

Final Test

Look at the coordinate plane and answer the questions. (15 marks)

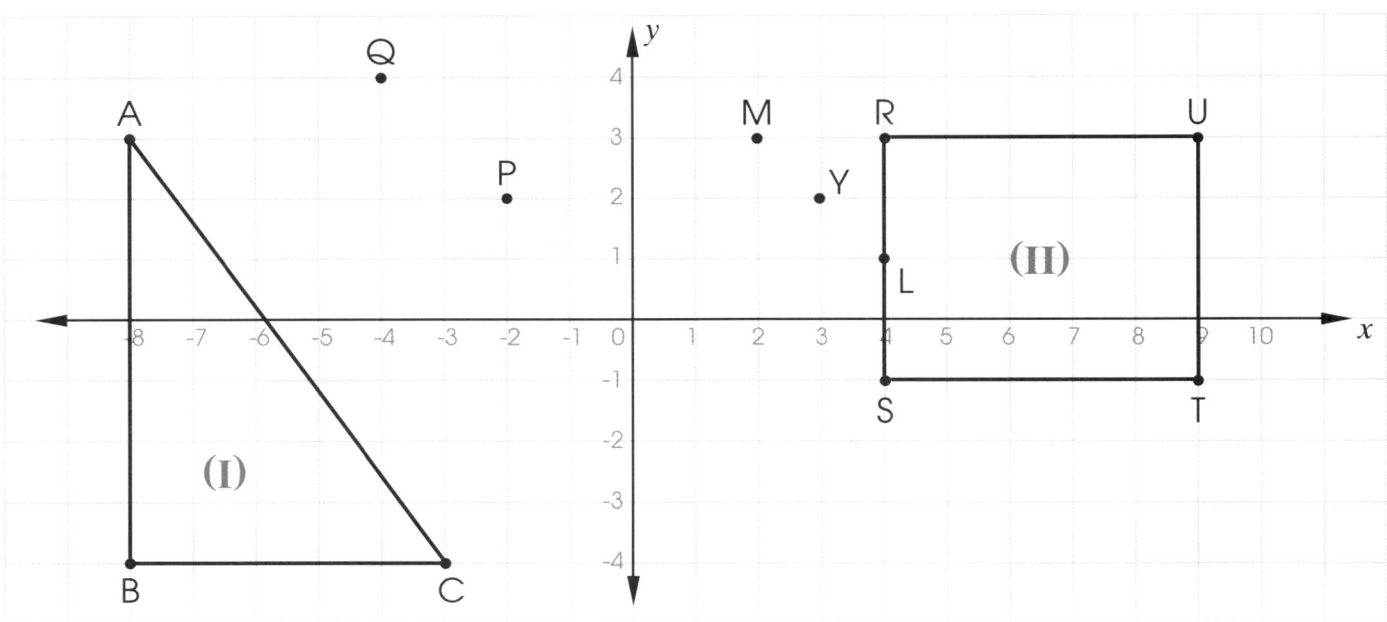

① Write the ordered pairs of the vertices of shape I.

A (___ , ___), B (___ , ___), C (___ , ___)

② Write the ordered pairs of the vertices of shape II.

R (___ , ___), S (___ , ___), T (___ , ___), U (___ , ___)

③ What is the area of shape I? _____ square units

④ What is the area of shape II? _____ square units

⑤ Which points are in the third quadrant? _____

⑥ Which points are in the fourth quadrant? _____

⑦ Dave is at (0, -2). If he moves 4 units up and 2 units left, he will reach point _____ .

⑧ Steve is at (1, 0). If he moves 1 unit up and 3 units right, he will reach point _____ .

66 MATHSMART (GRADE 7)

Write in algebraic expressions. (4 marks)

⑨ The sum of 4 and the square of x. _____

⑩ Subtract 16 from the product of y and 4. _____

⑪ 3 more than m times 9. _____

⑫ The difference of q and 5, divided by 4. _____

Evaluate for $p = 6$ and $q = -3$. (4 marks)

⑬ $4p + 2q$ = _____

⑭ $-2pq$ = _____

⑮ $(3p - 4) \times q$ = _____

⑯ $p^2 + q^2$ = _____

Simplify the expressions. (4 marks)

⑰ $3(a - b) + 4b$

= _____

⑱ $2(8 - m) + 5m$

= _____

⑲ $5(n + 7) - 2(n + 1)$

= _____

⑳ $2(t + 6) - 3(2t - 1)$

= _____

Solve the equations. (4 marks)

㉑ $6a - 3a - 0.5a = 9$

㉒ $3.5b - 20 = 11.5$

Final Test

Find the value of the angles. (16 marks)

㉓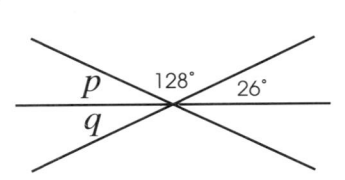

p = ____
q = ____

㉔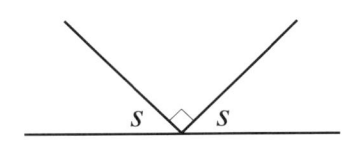

s = ____

㉕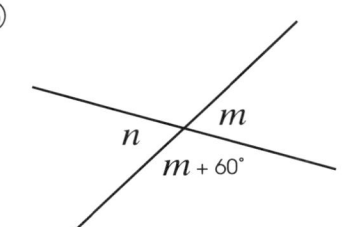

m = ____
n = ____

㉖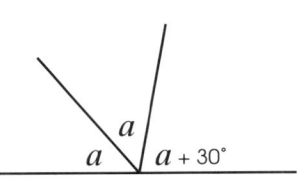

a = ____

㉗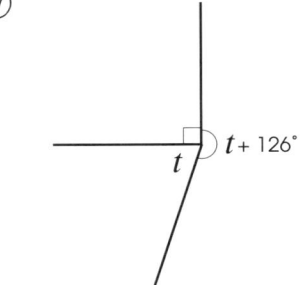

t = ____

㉘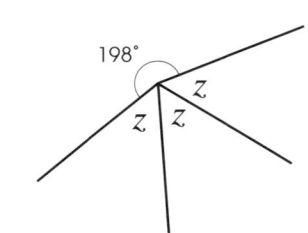

z = ____

㉙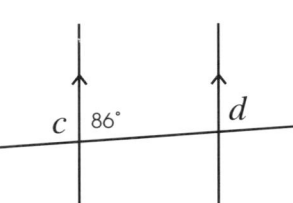

c = ____
d = ____

㉚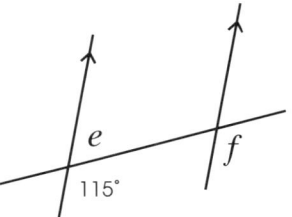

e = ____
f = ____

㉛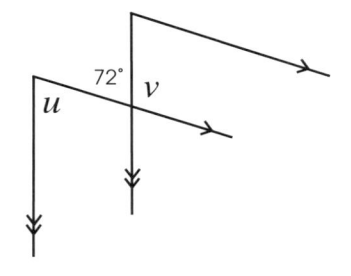

u = ____
v = ____

㉜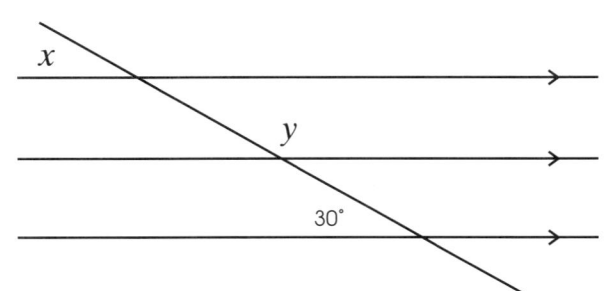

x = ____
y = ____

Write congruent or similar. (3 marks)

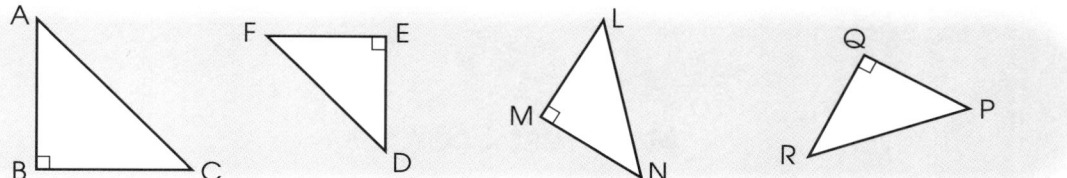

㉝ △ABC and △DEF are _____ triangles.

㉞ △LMN and △PQR are _____ triangles.

㉟ △DEF and △PQR are _____ triangles.

Find the third angle of each triangle. (4 marks)

㊱ 33°, 46°, _____   ㊲ 120°, 36°, _____

㊳ 98°, 37°, _____   ㊴ 49°, 52°, _____

Construct the following with a ruler and a pair of compasses only. (6 marks)

㊵ A perpendicular bisector for line segment PQ

㊶ An isosceles triangle with 2 sides 5 cm each and 1 side 6 cm

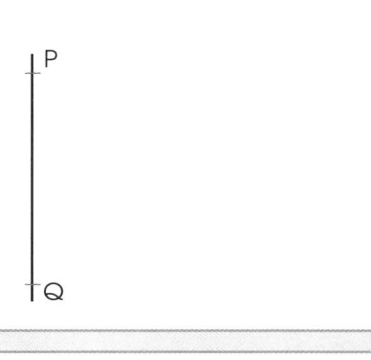

㊷ An angle bisector for ∠PQR

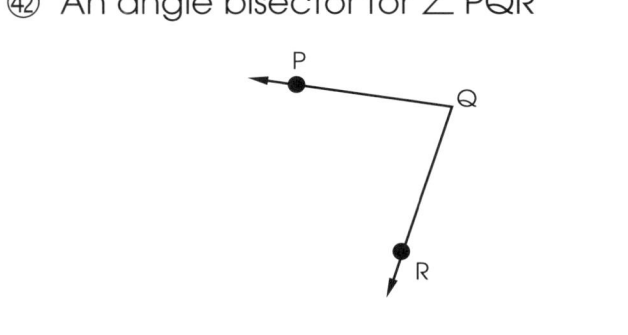

Final Test

Use the histogram to complete the frequency distribution table and answer the questions. (8 marks)

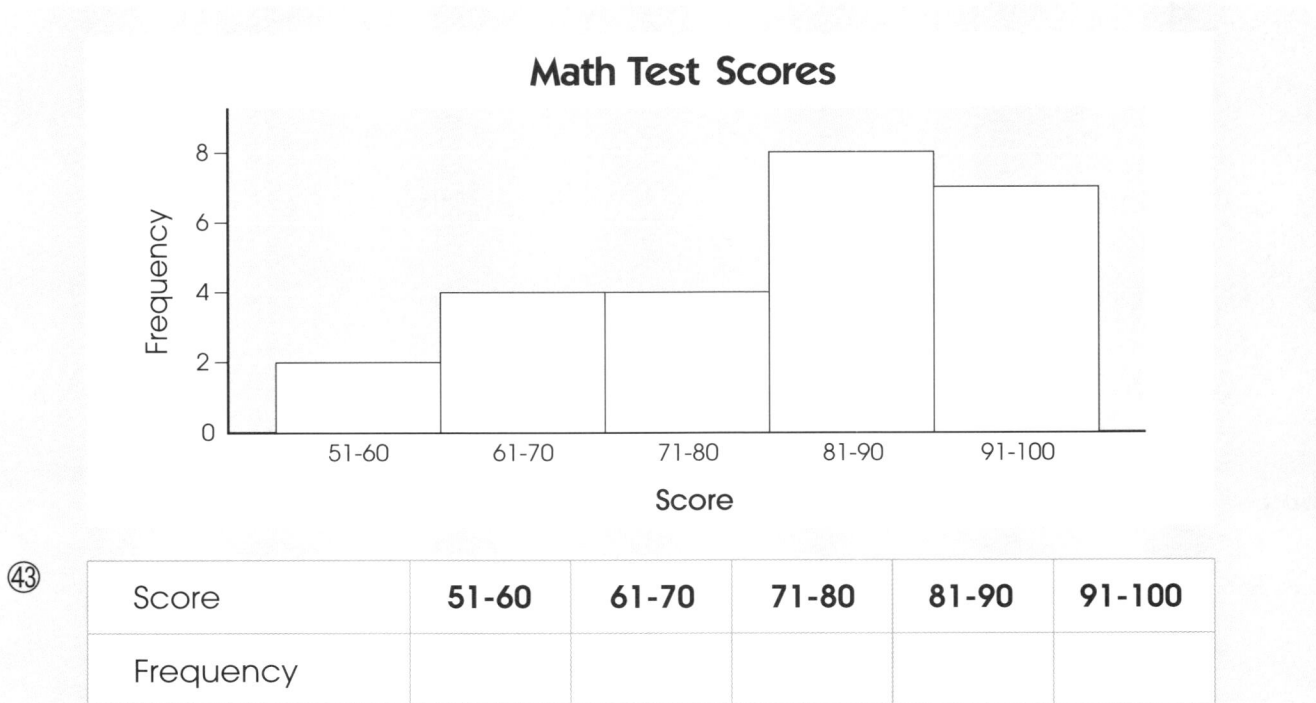

㊳
Score	51-60	61-70	71-80	81-90	91-100
Frequency					

㊹ How many students scored between 61 and 80? _____

㊺ How many students scored over 81? _____

㊻ How many students participated in the test? _____

Find the size of the angle for each group and complete the circle graph. (8 marks)

English Test Scores	Percent	Angle
0 - 19	12.5 %	45°
㊼ 20 - 39	12.5 %	
㊽ 40 - 59	30 %	
㊾ 60 - 79	25 %	
㊿ 80 - 100	20 %	

㊑ English Test Scores

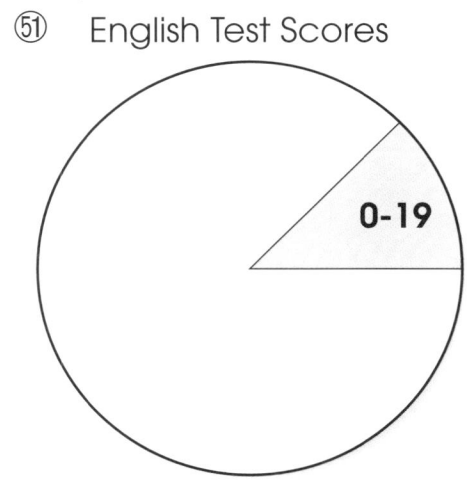

Draw each reflection image in the line *l*. (4 marks)

(52)

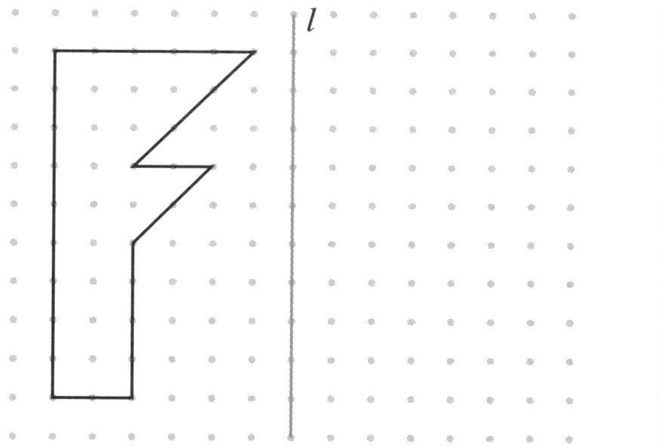

(53)

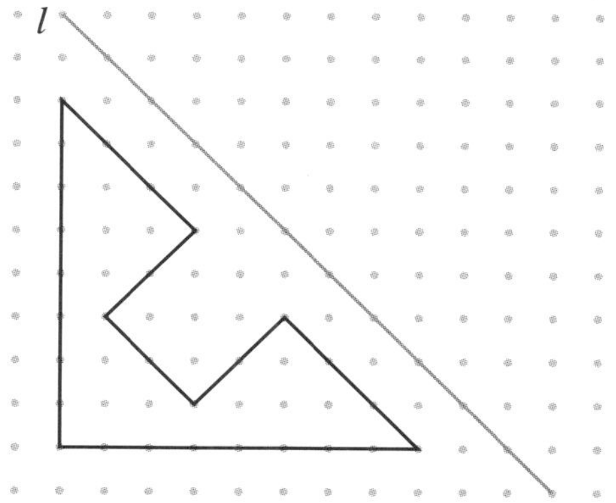

Describe the translation images of the shaded trapezoid. Write the numbers and tick ✔ the right boxes. (4 marks)

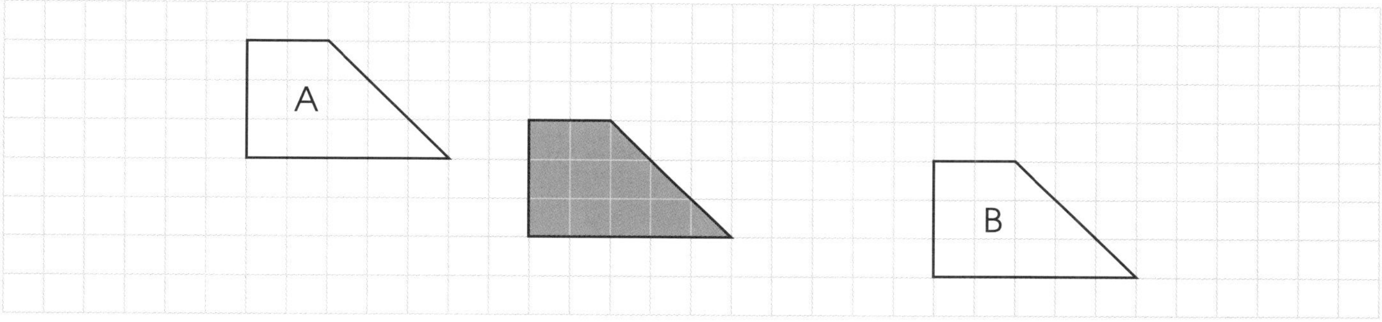

(54) Image A : ________ unit(s) to the ☐ left ☐ right and ________ unit(s) ☐ up ☐ down

(55) Image B : ________ unit(s) to the ☐ left ☐ right and ________ unit(s) ☐ up ☐ down

Find the coordinates of the turning point, angle and direction of rotation of each rotation image of the shaded triangle. (4 marks)

	Image	Turning Point	Angle and Direction of Rotation
(56)	A	(,)	
(57)	B	(,)	

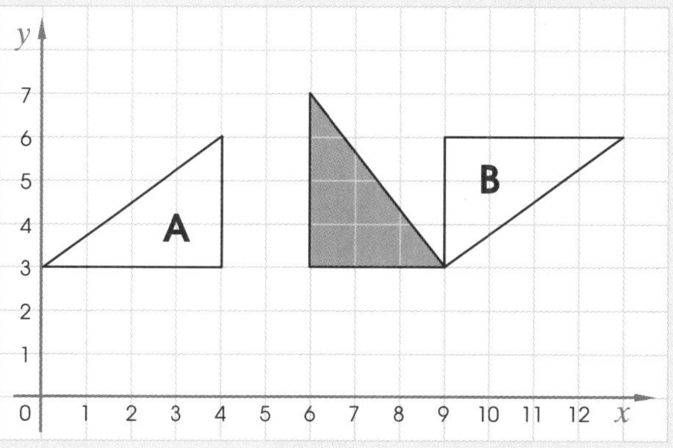

Final Test

Use the spinner below to find the probabilities. (6 marks)

⑤⑧ P(9) =

⑤⑨ P(6) =

⑥⓪ P (number less than 4) =

⑥① P (number greater than 10) =

⑥② P (even number) =

⑥③ P(1 or 9) =

List all the possible outcomes and probabilities. (6 marks)

⑥④ The spinner is spun twice.

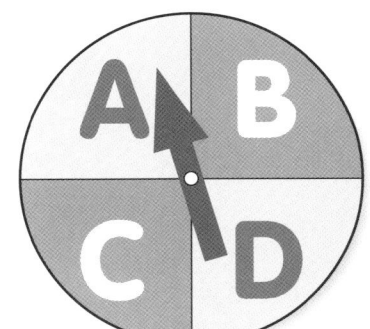

a. Possible outcomes : _____

_____

b. P (two letters are the same) = _____

c. P (one letter is B) = _____

⑥⑤ A coin is tossed 3 times. (H for head and T for tail)

a. Possible outcomes : _____

_____

b. P (exactly 2 heads) = _____

c. P (at least 2 tails) = _____

MathSmart ANSWERS 7

1 Number Theory

1. 2^3 Exponent = 3   Base = 2
2. 7^5 Exponent = 5   Base = 7
3. 9^6 Exponent = 6   Base = 9
4. 5^8 Exponent = 8   Base = 5
5. 625   6. 1   7. 9
8. 144   9. 64   10. 1
11. 13   12. 1   13. 216
14. 10^2 15. 10^5 16. 10^3
17. 10^4 18. 10^6 19. 10^5
20. 10^7 21. 1; 4; 6; 3
22. $3 \times 10^3 + 7 \times 10^1 + 5 \times 10^0$
23. $1 \times 10^2 + 5 \times 10^1 + 9 \times 10^0$
24. $4 \times 10^4 + 2 \times 10^3 + 6 \times 10^1 + 2 \times 10^0$
25. 21 432   26. 30 509   27. 600 332
28. 40 305

29.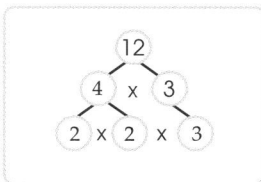

    $2 \times 2 \times 3$
    3

30.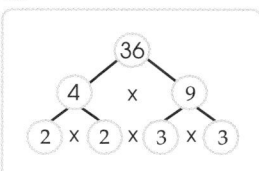

    $2 \times 2 \times 3 \times 3$
    $2^2 \times 3^2$

31.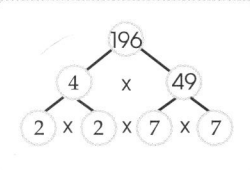

    $2 \times 2 \times 7 \times 7$
    $2^2 \times 7^2$

32.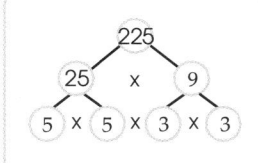

    $5 \times 5 \times 3 \times 3$
    $5^2 \times 3^2$

33. 4   34. 2   35. 2^6
36. 3×5^2 37. $2^4 \times 5^2$ 38. $2^3 \times 3 \times 5$
39. $2^2 \times 11^2$ 40. $2^3 \times 3^2$ 41. 3×5^3
42. $2^3 \times 5^2$
43. $2 \times 2 \times 2 \times 2$ 44. $3 \times 3 \times 7 \times 7$
    4   21
45. $2 \times 2 \times 5 \times 5$ 46. $2 \times 2 \times 11 \times 11$
    10   22
47. 16   48. 30
49. 12   50. 18

Activity
1. 25   2. 49

2 Algebraic Expressions

1. a. $8k + 4$ b. $8 \times 7 + 4 = 60$
2. a. $12m + 7$ b. $12 \times 5 + 7 = 67$
3. a. $5p + 3$ b. $5 \times 8 + 3 = 43$
4. 27   5. 90   6. 16
7. 75   8. 22   9. 36
10. 10   11. 7   12. 16
13. 9   14. 14   15. 8.7
16. 3.6   17. 0.8   18. 0.4
19. 6.3   20. 0   21. 1.6
22. 36   23. $3\frac{1}{2}$ 24. $\frac{3}{4}$
25. $\frac{2}{5}$ 26. 10   27. 15
28. 22   29. 5   30. 1
31. 3.5   32. 0   33. 0.25
34. 25   35. 1.2

36. a.
y	(x, y)
2	(0, 2)
4	(2, 4)
5	(3, 5)

    b. 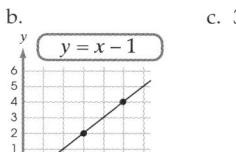 $y = x + 2$ c. 3

37. a.
y	(x, y)
0	(1, 0)
2	(3, 2)
4	(5, 4)

    b. $y = x - 1$ c. 3

38. a.
y	(x, y)
6	(0, 6)
4	(2, 4)
2	(4, 2)

    b. $y = 6 - x$ c. 3

39. a.
y	(x, y)
1	(2, 1)
2	(4, 2)
3	(6, 3)

    b. 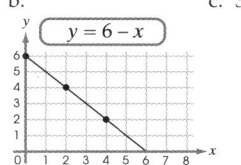 $y = x \div 2$ c. 4

Activity
1. 50; (1, 50)
   100; (2, 100)
   200; (4, 200)
   300; (6, 300)
2. $y = 50x$

3 Fractions

1. $3\frac{1}{2}$
2. 2
3. $21\frac{1}{4}$
4. $14\frac{1}{2}$
5. 48
6. 33
7. 30
8. $7\frac{7}{8}$
9. $1\frac{3}{4}$
10. 10
11. 4
12. $\frac{1}{6}$
13. $2\frac{2}{11}$
14. $4\frac{1}{6}$
15. 22
16. $\frac{7}{18}$
17. $2\frac{1}{3}$
18. $\frac{5}{6}$
19. $3\frac{3}{4}$
20. 4
21. $\frac{3}{7}$
22. $1\frac{2}{3}$
23. $1\frac{1}{2}$
24. 7
25. $\frac{1}{8}$
26. $\frac{5}{7}$
27. $\frac{1}{3}$
28. $\frac{4}{5}$
29. $\frac{6}{11}$
30. 6
31. climbing
32. $7\frac{1}{2} \div 3\frac{1}{3} = 2\frac{1}{4}$

    $2\frac{1}{4}$
33. $1\frac{1}{5} \times 3\frac{1}{3} = 4$

    4
34. $2\frac{1}{2} \times \frac{2}{3} = 1\frac{2}{3}$

    $1\frac{2}{3}$
35. $\frac{3}{4} \div 4 = \frac{3}{16}$

    $\frac{3}{16}$
36. $\frac{7}{8} - \frac{7}{8} \times \frac{2}{5} = \frac{21}{40}$

    $\frac{21}{40}$

Activity
1. $12\frac{3}{8}$
2. $18\frac{9}{16}$
3. $1\frac{1}{2}$

4 Percent

1. 36%
2. 62.5%
3. 42.86%
4. 68.75%
5. 180%
6. 285.71%
7. 126.67%
8. $\frac{1}{2}$
9. $\frac{23}{50}$
10. $\frac{6}{25}$
11. $\frac{2}{25}$
12. $\frac{1}{50}$
13. $\frac{39}{50}$
14. 45
15. 38.89
16. 37.5
17. 41.67
18. 37.5
19. 33.6
20. 162.5
21. 74.8
22. 24
23. 16.2
24. a. 18
    b. 24
    c. 78
25. 10
26. 30
27. 3.75
28. 5
29. $\frac{65}{250} \times 100\% = 26\%$

    26
30. 35.28
31. 62.06
32. 14.34
33. 62.99
34. 21.39
35. 24.15
36. 64.40
37. 26.44
38. 48.98
39. 44.03
40. 35%; $31.50
41. $75; 15%
42. 20%; $28.68
43. 7%; $42.80
44. $29.50; 12%
45. 6%; $4.95
46. 22.95
47. 35.55
48. 36.11

Activity
37.8

5 Measurement

1. 28; 40
2. 18; 20.25
3. 9.7; 2.75
4. 13.6; 3.96
5. 29; 30
6. 26.2; 15
7. 10.5
8. 8.85
9. 19
10. 35.85
11. 2.34
12. 393
13. 72
14. 140 000
15. 165 000
16. 84 500
17. 9 400 000
18. 126
19. 4.732
20. 4 x 3.8 x 49 = 744.80

    744.80
21. (4 x 2.5 x 2 + 3.8 x 2.5 x 2) ÷ 24 = 1.625

    2
22.
23. ✓
24. ✓
25.
26. 24
27. 360
28. 97.5
29. 324
30. 695.4
31. 12; 43.2
32. 17.5; 143.5
33. 10.5; 63
34. 6; 57
35. 6.3; 37.8
36. 18.36; 91.8
37. 27; 248.4
38. 2.356
39. 1.73
40. 0.36
41. 1 500 000
42. 7 000
43. 600 000
44. 1 040 000
45. 120 000; 0.12
46. 9.6

Activity
1. 6; 3; 0.5 x 6 - 1 + 3 = 5
2. 6; 4; 0.5 x 6 - 1 + 4 = 6

6 Approximation
1. A
2. E
3. A
4. E
5. A
6. 14.5
7. 9.5
8. 13.5
9. 13.5
10. 2 cm; 2.5 cm
11. 2 cm; 2 cm
12. 3 cm; 3.5 cm
13. 10 cm; 10 cm

Activity
Estimate: Individual answer
Exact: 30

7 Integers
1. a. +$1 200   b. -$450
2. a. +1 kg   b. -3 kg
3. <
4. <
5. <
6. >
7. >
8. <
9. -6, -3, 0, +2, +4
10. -4, -3, +1, +5, +7
11. -5, -1, 0, +3, +6
12. (+5) + (-8) = -3
13. (-2) + (+6) = +4
14. (-3) + (-4) = -7
15. (+6) + (+2) = +8
16. (+5) + (-5) = 0
17. -12
18. -5
19. -3
20. +12
21. 0
22. -4
23. +11
24. -5
25. -7
26. +4
27. +8
28. -6
29. -6
30. +7
31. -26
32. +20
33. +3
34. -4
35. +9
36. -10
37. (-5) + (+4)
    -1
38. (+4) + (-7)
    -3
39. (-13) + (-2)
    -15
40. (+6) + (+10)
    +16
41. +2
42. +11
43. +8
44. +22
45. -5
46. -4
47. +7
48. -8
49. -3
50. +1
51. +22
52. -54
53. -30
54. -5
55. +20
56. +5
57. -7
58. +3
59. -35
60. -20
61. Practice makes perfect.

Activity
1. Sunday
2. Tuesday
3. 9

8 Fractions, Decimals and Percent
1. 20%; $\frac{1}{5}$
2. 0.28; $\frac{7}{25}$
3. 45%; 0.45
4. 65%; $\frac{13}{20}$
5. 66.67%; 0.67
6. 140%; $1\frac{2}{5}$
7. 270%; 2.7
8. Dave; 1; Tony
9. Helen; 0.15; Elaine
10. 3; math; history
11. 11
12. 15
13. 4
14. 20
15. 3
16. 13.2
17. 18.9
18. 0.175
19. 0.74

20.

Dave White — MATH TEST
1. $2^2 \times 0.3 - 1$ = 0.2 ✓
2. $(14 - \frac{1}{2} \times 10)^2$ = 81 ✓
3. $7 - 0.65 \times 10$ = 63.5
4. $18 - \frac{1}{4} \times 12 \div 2$ = 7.5 ✓
5. $30\% \times (15 - 9)^2$ = 10.8 ✓
6. $(12 - 2) \times 6 - 4^2$ = 44 ✓
7. $\frac{7}{12} \times 144 - 6 \div 3$ = 82 ✓
8. $10 - (35\% \times 9 - 2)$ = 8.85 ✓
GRADE: $\frac{6}{8}$ = 75 %

21.

Steve Lindsay — MATH TEST
1. $3^2 \times (15 - 12)$ = 27 ✓
2. $20 + 6 \times 3 \div 2$ = 29 ✓
3. $(4 + 5)^2 - 10 \times$ = 76 ✓
4. $(40 - 26) \div 2 - 7$ = 0 ✓
5. $(0.2 + 50\%) \times 6^2$ = 25.2 ✓
6. $(0.5 + 5) \times 2^2$ = 121
7. $\frac{2}{5} \times 45 - 16 \times 80\%$ = 5.2 ✓
8. $(25 - 9) \div 4 + 50\% \times 6$ = 27
GRADE: $\frac{6}{8}$ = 75 %

22. a. 547.25   b. 584
23. a. 9.03   b. 10.19
24. a. 325   b. 220
25. a. 24   b. 34.60

Activity
1. 5 x 2 + 4 - 3 - 1 = 10
2. 3 x (2 + 1) + 5 - 4 = 10
3. 5 x 2 x 1 x (4 - 3) = 10
4. ((4 x 2) - 5) x 3 + 1 = 10

Midway Test
1. 8^{12} Exponent = 12   Base = 8
2. 4^5 Exponent = 5   Base = 4
3. 3^4; 9
4. 2^4; 4
5. 2^6; 8
6. $2^4 \times 5^2$; 20
7. $2^2 \times 7^2$; 14
8. $2^2 \times 11^2$; 22

9. 4   10. 21   11. 8.8
12. 1.3   13. 25   14. 0.54
15. 1.2   16. 2   17. $1\frac{1}{3}$
18. $15\frac{1}{2}$ 19. 3   20. $\frac{3}{10}$
21. $\frac{4}{5}$ 22. 2   23. $\frac{1}{2}$
24. $\frac{1}{3}$ 25. 8   26. $\frac{7}{12}$
27. 104   28. 41.67   29. 25
30. $10; $30   31. $22.50; $52.50
32. $126; 20%   33. 15%; $75.82
34. $4.32; $40.32   35. 8%; $16.74
36. $75.60; 15%
37. $31\frac{1}{2}$; $40\frac{5}{8}$ 38. 20.8; 20
39. 33.8; 43.7   40. 15.8; 16.12
41. 28.8   42. 2   43. 29.5
44. 72   45. 0.52   46. 18 500
47. 4.56   48. 850 000
49. 5 cm; 5 cm   50. 8 cm; 8.5 cm
51. 13 cm; 12.5 cm   52. -11
53. -21 ÷ -3 = 7   54. 4 − 12 = -8
55. -12 x 6 = -72   56. -6 x 3 = -18
57. -12 ÷ -6 = 2   58. -21 + 3 −(-12) = -6
59. 5 − (-6 + 14) = -3
60. y + 12 = +5   61. x = 7 − 11
    y = -7   x = -4
    -7   -4
62. $1\frac{3}{5}$; 160%   63. 0.45; $\frac{9}{20}$
64. Dave's savings = $70 x 38.5% = $26.95
    Steve's savings = $50 x 46.3% = $23.15
    Dave; 3.80; Steve
65. a. 80 x 85% = 68   b. $\frac{72}{80}$ x 100% = 90%
       68   90
66. a. 33   b. 0.50

9 Coordinates

1. (0, 10)   2. (6, 10)   3. (8, 10)
4. (14, 10)   5. (1, 8)   6. (3, 8)
7. (16, 8)   8. (2, 7)   9. (4, 7)
10. (5, 5)   11. (11, 5)   12. (18, 0)
13. I   14. C   15. G
16. K   17. (-6, -3)   18. (0, -3)
19. (4, 3)   20. (5, 5)   21. (-4, -2)
22. (3, -5)   23. (-3, 5)   24. (-4, 2)
25. B, C, F, H   26. A, D, G   27. L, N, R
28. M, Q, S   29. I, J, K   30. E, J, P
31. B(-6, 3), C(-6, -5), D(-8, -5)
32. E(2, 3), F(5, 3), G(7, -1), H(2, -1)
33. L(-3, -1), M(-3, -5), N(1, -5)
34. a. 2   b. 8   c. 16
35. a. 3   b. 5   c. 4
    d. 16
36. a. 4   b. 4   c. 8
37. a.

y	-1	2	4
(x, y)	(0, -1)	(3, 2)	(5, 4)

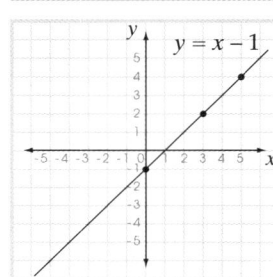

b. 3   c. 2

38. a.

y	-3	1	5
(x, y)	(-1, -3)	(1, 1)	(3, 5)

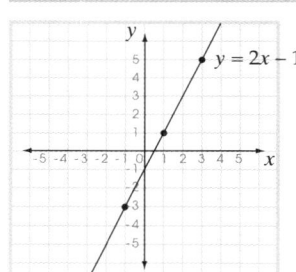

b. 3   c. 0

Activity
1. y = x + 2   2. x = 1   3. (1, 3)

10 More about Algebraic Expressions

1. $y^2 − 25$ 2. $(25 + y) ÷ 5$
3. $25 + y^2$ 4. $(y − 25)^2$ or $(25 − y)^2$
5. $(25 + y) \times 2$ 6. $25y − 25$
7. 24   8. 42   9. 36
10. 0.9   11. 12   12. -11
13. 0   14. 8

15. $5x^2$, $3x$, $2y$, -8; 4
16. $3a$, $2b$, -6; 3
17. $0.5m$, $2n$, $-2p$, 9; 4
18. $8u^3$, $-4u^2$, 3; 3
19. like
20. unlike
21. like
22. unlike
23. $10p + 4$
24. $6d + 13$
25. $-9k - 9$
26. $1\frac{1}{4}m - 7$
27. $15n^2 - 10n + 5$
28. $-6a + 3b + 4$
29. $9m - 4n + 5$
30. $-4pq$
31. $5x^2y + 2y$
32. $3x + 9$
33. $3y - 2$
34. $8h - 12$
35. $-2m - 4$
36. $4n + 12$
37. $5p + 8$
38. 15
39. 7
40. 36
41. 0
42. -8
43. 11
44. 8
45. -1
46. 15.6
47. -2.2
48. 6.6
49. 0.2
50. a. 18   b. 60   c. 16   d. 384
51. a. 45   b. 36   c. 360   d. 10
52. a. 60   b. 100   c. 14   d. 0.3
53. a. 87.5%   b. 32.5%   c. 93.75%   d. 80%
54. $8y = 16$
    $8y \div 8 = 16 \div 8$
    $y = 2$
    Check: $3(2) + 5(2) = 16$
55. $x - 3 = 6$
    $x - 3 + 3 = 6 + 3$
    $x = 9$
    Check: $(9) - 7 + 4 = 6$
56. $2m = -12$
    $2m \div 2 = -12 \div 2$
    $m = -6$
    Check: $8(-6) - 6(-6) = -12$
57. $2a = 14$
    $2a \div 2 = 14 \div 2$
    $a = 7$
    Check: $8(7) - 12(7) + 6(7) = 14$
58. $3y + 14 = 38$
    $3y + 14 - 14 = 38 - 14$
    $3y = 24$
    $3y \div 3 = 24 \div 3$
    $y = 8$
    8
59. $4 \times m + 20 = 100$
    $4m + 20 - 20 = 100 - 20$
    $4m = 80$
    $4m \div 4 = 80 \div 4$
    $m = 20$
    20
60. $8 \times 5 \times p = 500$
    $40p = 500$
    $40p \div 40 = 500 \div 40$
    $p = 12.50$
    12.50

Activity

11 Angles and Lines

1. 30°; 90°; adjacent
2. 30°; 30°; opposite
3. 30°; 60°; complementary
4. 30°; 150°; supplementary
5. 37°
6. 34°
7. 95°
8. 53°
9. 45°; 80°
10. 30°; 90°
11. 45°; 55°
12. 30°
13. 110°
14. 67°
15. 156°; 24°
16. 100°; 35°
17. 78°; 102°
18. corresponding
19. alternate
20. alternate
21. corresponding
22. 120°; 60°
23. 100°; 80°
24. 125°; 125°
25. 54°; 126°
26. 135°; 135°
27. 145°; 35°
28. 61°; 119°
29. 25°; 45°
30. 40°; 45°
31. 122°; 58°
32. 80°; 42°
33. 60°; 65°
34. 60°; 96°
35. 124°; 56°
36. 58°; 50°

Activity

1. AB
2. same

12 Angles and Shapes

1. 60°; 60°; 60°
   180°
   Equilateral
2. 130°; 25°; 25°
   180°
   Isosceles
3. 80°; 70°; 30°
   180°
   Scalene
4. 95°
5. 29°
6. 16°
7. 84°
8. 40°
9. 25°
10. 48°
11. 71°
12. 95°
13. 90°
14. 52°
15. 45°

16.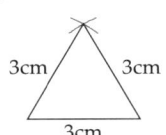
17.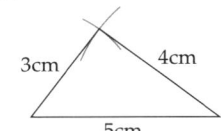
18.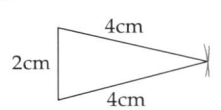
19.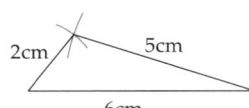
20.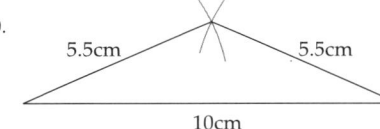
21.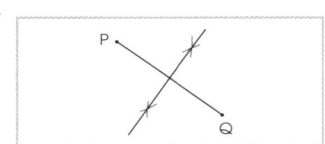
22.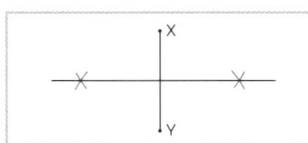
23.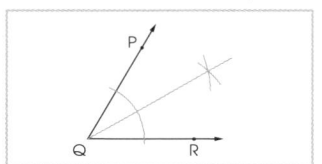
24.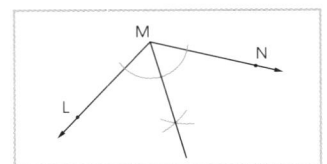

25. congruent
26. similar
27. similar
28. congruent

Activity
1. 2; 3
2. 8; 16

13 Statistics

1. 2 500
2. 2 000
3. March
4. April
5. 45
6. 10
7. 20
8. 72°
9. 90°
10. 54°
11. 36°

12.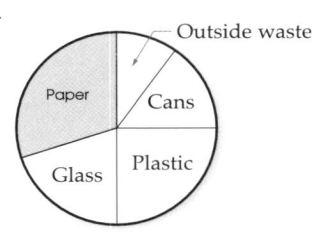

13. 30
14. 25
15. 10
16. 80
17. 2; 3; 7; 5; 13

18.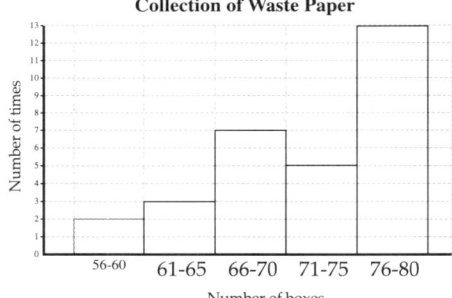

19. Number of times
20. Number of boxes
21. 30 weeks

Activity
   B

14 Transformations

1.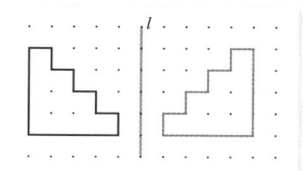

2.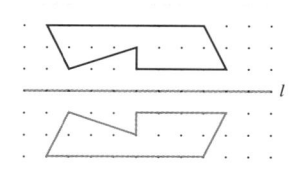

3. 5 units right and 2 units up
4. 5 units left and 3 units down
5. 3 units down
6. 7 units right and 3 units down
7. (5,4); 90°, counter clockwise
8. (6, 1); 90°, counter clockwise
9. (11, 3); 180°, counter clockwise or clockwise

Activity
4; 8; 5; 6

15 Probability

1. $\frac{2}{8}$ ($\frac{1}{4}$)
2. $\frac{2}{8}$ ($\frac{1}{4}$)
3. $\frac{3}{8}$
4. $\frac{2}{8}$ ($\frac{1}{4}$)
5. $\frac{3}{8}$
6. $\frac{1}{8}$
7. $\frac{3}{8}$
8. $\frac{2}{8}$ ($\frac{1}{4}$)
9. $\frac{1}{8}$
10. $\frac{2}{8}$ ($\frac{1}{4}$)
11. $\frac{5}{8}$
12. $\frac{4}{8}$ ($\frac{1}{2}$)
13. $\frac{7}{8}$
14. a. 9 b. $\frac{3}{9}$ ($\frac{1}{3}$)
    c. $\frac{4}{9}$
15. a. 12 b. $\frac{1}{12}$
    c. $\frac{1}{12}$ d. $\frac{2}{12}$ ($\frac{1}{6}$)
    e. $\frac{2}{12}$ ($\frac{1}{6}$)

Activity
1. A $\frac{3}{8}$ B $\frac{1}{4}$
   C $\frac{1}{5}$
2. A

Final Test
1. A(-8, 3), B(-8, -4), C(-3, -4)
2. R(4, 3), S(4, -1), T(9, -1), U(9, 3)
3. 17.5 4. 20
5. B, C 6. S, T
7. P 8. L
9. $4 + x^2$ 10. $4y - 16$
11. $9m + 3$ 12. $(q - 5) \div 4$ or $(5 - q) \div 4$
13. 18 14. 36
15. -42 16. 45
17. $3a + b$ 18. $16 + 3m$
19. $3n + 33$ 20. $-4t + 15$
21. $2.5a = 9$ 22. $3.5b = 31.5$
    $a = 3.6$ $b = 9$
23. 26°; 26° 24. 45°
25. 60°; 60° 26. 50°
27. 72° 28. 54°
29. 94°; 86° 30. 65°; 115°
31. 72°; 108° 32. 30°; 150°
33. similar 34. congruent
35. congruent 36. 101°
37. 24° 38. 45°
39. 79°
40.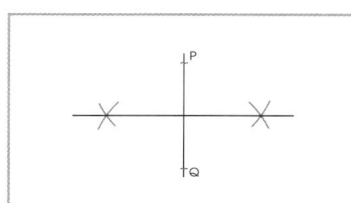
41.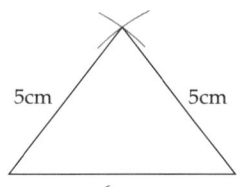

42.
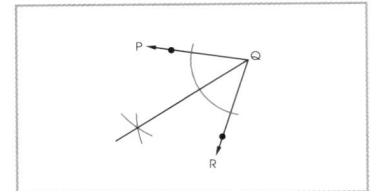

65. a. HHH, HHT, HTH, HTT, THH, TTH, THT, TTT
    b. $\frac{3}{8}$ c. $\frac{4}{8}$ ($\frac{1}{2}$)

43. 2; 4; 4; 8; 7   44. 8
45. 15   46. 25
47. 45°   48. 108°
49. 90°   50. 72°

51.
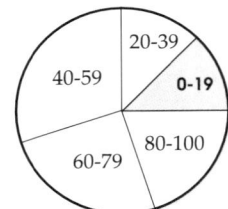

52.
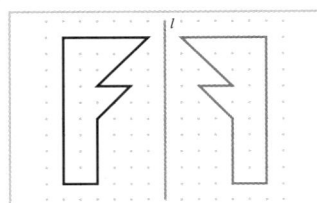

53.
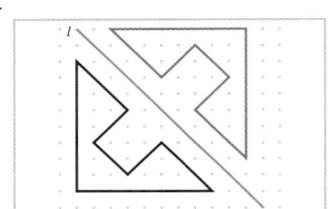

54. 7; left; 2; up   55. 10; right; 1; down
56. (5, 2); 90° counter clockwise
57. (9, 3); 90° clockwise

58. $\frac{3}{10}$ 59. $\frac{2}{10}$ ($\frac{1}{5}$)
60. $\frac{2}{10}$ ($\frac{1}{5}$)   61. 0
62. $\frac{4}{10}$ ($\frac{2}{5}$)   63. $\frac{4}{10}$ ($\frac{2}{5}$)

64. a. AA, AB, AC, AD, BB, BA, BC, BD, CA, CB, CC, CD, DA, DB, DC, DD

    b. $\frac{4}{16}$ ($\frac{1}{4}$)   c. $\frac{7}{16}$